How to Become a Brilliant Leader

Leadership Lessons from Lilly, The Best Dog Coach a Leader Could Ask For!

Carla Howard

CONTENTS

INTRODUCTION

Leadership has been my professional passion for over 25 years. This has led me to devour countless books, articles, and TED Talks on the topic. I've been incredibly fortunate to learn the art first-hand from brilliant and gifted leaders. Their patience, focus on developing others, and grace under pressure have provided excellent examples to follow. Thankfully, the vast majority of my professional life I've had the good fortune to work for great leaders. The lessons I learned from them helped me to survive on the rare occasion when people in charge were oppressive or unkind.

Learning can be painful. I wouldn't trade any of these experiences because they have culminated into a successful career as an international change leader, coach, mentor, facilitator, and trainer. I thought I'd pretty much cracked the code to being a great leader… and then along came Lilly.

Lilly is an adorable Vizsla we've had since she was eight weeks old. She brings loads of energy, love, and a bit of exasperation into our home. As my husband Jeff and I took Lilly to obedience classes and put in hours of teaching at home, I began drawing a clear correlation between training this new addition to our family and leading people. The similarities were striking. I was becoming a more patient leader as a result of focusing on patience with Lilly. Entering every training session with a positive state of mind and expecting Lilly to do well was critical. She knew when I was frustrated, even when doing my best to hide it. Focusing on a better approach with Lilly created other personal changes. I observed more keenly, listened fully, and became more committed to showing more appreciation to people in my life. I became a better leader through the experience of training our dog.

We take on many leadership roles during our lifetimes. Thankfully, the vast majority of leaders are good people doing their best to balance business and employee needs. Learning how to be the best parent, spouse, friend, colleague, dog mom, or business leader requires us to be on a continuous self-improvement journey. Because the most significant results are usually created from small changes in approach, it's not necessary to make dozens of changes at one time.

Implement a few of the leadership tips and pieces of advice from these pages that work best with your personal style, then see the results for yourself.

Who could have guessed a precocious puppy would become a patient and kind leadership coach? This book outlines the lessons I've learned from Lilly, and provides practical advice on how you can incorporate them into your journey to become a brilliant leader!

Do you need a mentor?

I've been fortunate to have several amazing mentors during my career. Their guidance made a huge impact on my professional development, so I decided many years ago that I would never say no when approached to be a mentor. Lately, saying yes to every request has become quite challenging. I had to find a way to say yes to more people. The Professional Woman's Mentor was launched to do just that. Check out options for individual mentoring, speaking engagements, and online mentoring courses at:

TheProfessionalWomansMentor.com

Or you can Email me at

Carla@TheProfessionalWomansMentor.com

CHAPTER ONE

Cultural Fit

Lilly:

"I love to be near my parents and Chaos (my big brother chocolate lab)!!! I love it so much that I am ALWAYS with them! I sit between dad's legs while he cooks, lay in mom's lap when she works from home, and my favorite place to sleep is right on top of Chaos. I can be found following my people every second of the day. Sitting on the couch? You guessed it! I'll be the one laying right beside them. Well, to be completely honest, I prefer to sprawl across their legs, but sometimes I have to settle for my head in a lap. I am always touching my people and Chaos. I just can't get close enough!

I wouldn't be happy if I didn't have constant contact and interaction with my family. It's a good thing they also like to be near me too or we would all be miserable."

Training Lilly:

Vizslas are called "Velcro Vizslas" for a reason!! Lilly is always connected to us. My husband Jeff and I knew this was a hallmark of the breed when we decided to add Lilly to our family. We did a great deal of research to make sure we were adding a family member who would be happy in our environment, and one we would enjoy spending the next 12 - 15 years with. If you don't want a dog that follows you everywhere you go and needs to be by your side every moment of the day… well, don't bring home a Vizsla!

The need to be physically close to us is one of Lilly's strongest personality traits, and is as much a part of her breading as swimming, pointing, and retrieving. I couldn't train the desire to be attached to us out of her, nor would I want to. While she is the perfect fit for our family, her need for constant contact would be frustrating for families with different needs and expectations of their canine companion.

Finding the right cultural fit is important when

choosing family pets, or adding new humans to work teams!

Lilly's Leadership Lesson:

Hiring is tricky business!! Sure, it's important to find a candidate with the technical skills needed to do the work. Just remember, those technical skills come in many different packages. I'll always make an offer to the candidate with the right blend of personality, patience, and a communication style that fits with my team over a person with excellent technical skills. The technical stuff can be taught. Better results are achieved by bringing on a new team member who is eager to learn, complements the personality of a team, and has a focus on value over a candidate with superb technical skills who may create negative disruptions.

Selecting the right addition to your team is challenging, hence the many articles and books on the topic. There are people who would be fabulous additions, but don't perform well in interviews. These folks rarely get the chance to join high-performing teams because they don't make it through the formal process. Then there are the "Super Stars" who WOW us during interviews only to become gigantic disappointments after a few months on the job. Adding technical skills at the expense of destroying team morale is a poor trade off at best. A slight shift in focus during the candidate search and interview processes will help build strong teams by hiring the right person the first time.

Define the (ideal) team culture

Clearly defining an ideal team culture is the best place to start. This typically will not be a posted statement on the team SharePoint site; however, the vision should be crystal clear to the members and felt by everyone they interact with. A clearly defined vision will be the North Star for all decision-making. The culture that is right for my business and leadership style may be very different from the elements you will need in order to create value in your business. As an example, support groups in sales driven organizations cannot survive without a clear focus on value delivery. In this environment, it would be important to add team members who thrive in a support role. For other opportunities, the ideal candidate may need one or more of the following attributes to be successful:

- Enjoy busy and creative collaboration
- Comfortable presenting to large audiences
- Perform with little direction
- Perform within strict guidelines

Being successful in hiring the right talent requires clear understanding of the traits needed for each opportunity. Answering these questions is helpful when struggling to define the ideal work environment:

Decision making process - Are most decisions made at the leadership level and passed down the line, or is a collaborative approach applied that includes members of the team?

Work from home and flexible schedules - Are these options? If yes, are they structured and rigid or are they flexible? What is the expectation for working after hours and on the weekend?

Dress code - What is the stated dress code, and equally important; what is the unofficial dress code? What do executives and senior leaders wear?

Office space - Do employees sit in cubicles while their leaders work from offices behind closed doors? Does everyone work in an open collaborative space? Is working from an outdoor space on company property an option?

Be very honest when assessing culture. It's easy to think, "We don't expect people to work more than a 40 hour work week. Evenings and weekends are an employee's personal time!", when in truth there is pressure to check email throughout the weekend or during vacation. Be aware of the differences between personal choices and what the company expects when assessing expectations. Don't project personal decisions as an expectation of the company.

Now that there is a clear mental picture of the culture an employee will hire into, frame interview questions and structure the hiring process to attract the right talent.

Likability

A vast majority of work is accomplished through influence. Likability is important because it's virtually impossible to be influenced by people we don't like. It's true. Think about colleagues and friends who are highly influential. This list may include direct leaders, colleagues, parents, pastors, neighbors, significant others, siblings, mentors, or coaches. I'll bet they are all people you like, which is very different from saying they are friends. Here is how to define the intangible quality of likability, and what to look for during the interview process to make sure likable people are joining the team:

Pleasing voice – Voice qualities are one of the first attributes noticed when engaging with others. Passion and excitement for the work can be heard and felt through vocal variety, an engaging tone, and confident responses. Shaky voices, whispers, or responses that are too loud are warning signs.

Value Focus - Who doesn't like people who want to help them be successful? During the interview, it's refreshing to hear candidates talk about how they have helped others succeed. Adding value to customers, colleagues, and organizations they are associated with is a hallmark of likable people. Employees are more successful and respected when they focus on meeting the needs of others.

Authentic Listening - Great listeners are naturally curious. They hear nuances in questions, answer inquiries directly, and often have interesting follow-up questions of their own. Authentic listeners never fiddle with their phones or answer an incoming call during conversations. They put everything else aside to focus on the current conversation. The best listeners actually appear as though they are listening with their eyes. We like people who show a genuine interest in how we feel and what we are saying. There is very little chance a candidate will be a great listener on the job if you don't see this attribute during the interview.

Sense of fun – Likable people can often be found coordinating team builders and celebrations. They find creative ways to thank colleagues for a job well done and show appreciation often. Engaging with people in a positive and appealing way is how they use influence to get work done. Look for candidates who share a fun side of their personality and are able to weave that into how it helps them accomplish great things at work.

Not afraid to make mistakes - Objectives cannot be achieved if team members don't feel safe or are unwilling to push the limits, try new ideas, and operate within guidelines without supervision. When I'm interviewing someone for an opening you can be sure one of the questions on the script will be something like "Tell me about your most recent (biggest, most high profile, etc.) mistake and what you learned from that experience". Proceed with caution if the candidate:

- Doesn't have a mistake they are willing to share.
- Gives an example where others made a mistake.
- Provides a scenario that describes his or her contribution in a positive light. An example of this would be a story about how the candidate

worked a 14-hour day to complete a task, and the lesson learned was to ask for help in the future. I'd much rather hear about a time where the candidate made a poor decision and what they learned from that experience.

- Doesn't share what was learned from the event.

Hire someone willing to push so far that mistakes will happen, and who has the courage to share mistakes openly so everyone can learn from the experience.

Other attributes - Also important are eye contact, a solid handshake, a genuine smile, and a confident vibe that comes from being at ease. Fidgety people who avoid eye contact typically won't fall in the "likable" category.

Stay on script

Create a standard set of questions to be asked of every applicant and stick to it. Using a script doesn't eliminate opportunities to ask clarifying questions or deviate based on what you learn. Be sure to document all answers and save the notes of every person on the interview panel. Documentation will come in handy if the interviewee asks for feedback on why an offer wasn't presented, or seeks legal counsel due to suspected discrimination or unfair hiring practices.

Be thoughtful about the interview script. Candidate answers, along with observations during the interview, will produce critical data the team will need to make the best selection. Include a few questions that should prompt creative responses. These answers will often help differentiate candidates in a close race. If you don't have standard preferred questions, a little bit of Internet research will provide dozens of great ideas. A few of my favorites are:

- If you had to describe yourself in one word, what would it be and why?
- What has been your biggest career mistake, and what did you learn from the experience?
- Describe a time you faced an ethical dilemma at work and how you handled the situation.
- Describe a time when you had to quickly remove yourself from a situation. What caused the situation, and how well did your solution work?

Use your best listening skills while candidates respond. It's quite common for people to share much more than you ask. It's rude to interrupt people during a response, and there is a good chance valuable information will be missed.

Make sure you get an answer to the question asked. This is a hot spot for me, as I am not pleased when a candidate doesn't answer a direct question. If this happens, follow-up with a second chance by asking something like "I'd really like to go back to my original question, can you provide a specific example of when……?". A great candidate will get the hint and provide a strong answer on the second pass.

Check out Social Media

Yes, I'm advocating being snoopy. Be VERY snoopy! Check slightly different spellings of candidates name (young people do this all the time on Facebook to hide from their parents) and research multiple sites. Don't forget to include LinkedIn, Tumblr, Instagram, Facebook, Pinterest, YouTube and other social sites. If it's on the World Wide Web, its fair game! Here are few things you can find out from a few quick searches:

Communications skills - LinkedIn is a good site to get a glimpse into writing skills. Take a look at profiles, posts, and articles written by the candidate. Articles provide insight into the writers' use of proper grammar, sentence structure, and the ability to communicate clear and concise messages.

Professional Passion - Which articles do they like, share, or comment on? Again, articles and posts written by the candidate are especially helpful. The content will reveal preferences related to work culture, management styles, career aspirations, and much more.

Personal Brand - Integrity, trustworthiness, and good decision-making are important in business. A quick look at personal social media accounts can tell you very quickly if the candidate's personal brand is one you want associated with your company or team. Let's face it, if you can find it on the Internet, so can your customers, competitors, and team members.

To help keep out of legal trouble, follow these tips:

- Be conscious that you are not basing hiring decisions on protected characteristics, because discrimination can be unconscious. You may learn about a candidates' age, disabilities, religion, sexual orientation, and other information that cannot be used to vet a candidate. Be sure you understand employment laws and abide by the guidelines. A better option would be to ask HR partners to conduct online research. They are skilled in what to look for and can share any concerns or positive feedback with the hiring manager.
- Conduct online searches only after you've met the candidate in person. Base the decision to interview solely on the resume and phone screening.
- Perform the same Internet research for all potential candidates. Basically, this is a different

type of an interview. Best practices recommend asking all candidates the same questions during interviews, and online searches are no different.

- Keep copies of the screen shots that help you make a hiring decision. Add the documentation to the applicants' portfolio and keep the information per your company's retention policy.

Here's the good news, a search of social media sites doesn't just uncover negative information. Interviewers often learn great things about prospective new employees that support a decision to hire!

Involve your team in the interviews process

Schedule time for everyone on your team to meet potential candidates. Difficulty matching schedules may require team members to conduct a few phone discussions in addition to the more formal in person interviews. Take the extra time necessary for each team member to talk with candidates and listen to employee feedback. Pay very close attention to that last bit... really listen to current employees' observations, concerns, and positive comments. It can be difficult to listen fully when there is a front-runner in mind, but it's actually even more important when a clear favorite exists. Other people will see things you don't. Be on guard that bias doesn't lead to adding someone who won't blend with your group.

One way to involve the team is to invite a candidate to have lunch with the group. It's still an interview, but in a much more casual setting. Don't have time to get away to a restaurant or the budget to do so? No problem!! Invite the candidate into the office for lunch, or just ask them to come by for coffee and pastries at the start of the day. A bit of informal chitchat is a good way to get to know people, and it will often bring out information and attitudes that don't surface in a more formal interview. We once had a front running candidate in for lunch and he spent the majority of the time complaining about his current boss, the leadership incompetency of the executive team, and his workload. None of this surfaced during the more formal panel interview! A plate of sandwiches, some lemonade, and a few bags of chips was all it took to open the floodgates. That lunch saved us from making a poor hiring decision. I'd say that was money and time well spent!

Don't use personality / behavioral tests

It is human nature to give preference to candidates we like, or those who express views similar to ours. Personality and behavioral assessments are generally used to neutralize this tendency. While I applaud the idea of using a bit of data in the hiring process, tests are not the best way to gather it. The ideas listed earlier in this chapter will provide all of the information needed to hire the best candidates. Here's why I don't recommend personality tests

People will say what they think you want to hear – I realize this also happens during interviews. The difference is that during the interview process there is an opportunity to hear a response while observing body language, tone of voice, and other warning signs that a bit of fibbing may be going on.

Evil twins - The "positive" attributes that come out in personality tests may have an evil twin… and we often forget that both will show up at work. Here's an example: A professional who earns high marks in being driven and goal-oriented may look like the perfect fit; however, evil twin attributes could include a tendency to be intimidating, a poor listener, and a bit of a bulldozer in the workplace. EEEK! That's not what you were looking for at all.

Preferences reinforced - Behavioral tests are often used to avoid hiring based on personal preferences or choosing people "like me". Here's the thing, I believe the opposite is true. Here's an example:

If I'm hiring for an executive role and feel confident that the best leaders are extroverts, great candidates who are categorized as introverts may be screened out of the process. Exceptional employees come in all packages. Don't push aside talent because test scores don't fit perceptions of an ideal profile.

Legal trouble - Check out the legalities around the administration and analysis of personality tests before making the decision to use them for candidate screening. Make sure there is a top notch HR team taking the lead because it's possible to wind up in hot water pretty darn quickly!

When you are the candidate

Now, let's talk about what to keep in mind when you are a candidate in the interview experience. Maintaining composure and professionalism can be difficult if you find interviews to be extremely stressful, or when the opportunity is particularly exciting. Here are a few tips to help make connections and leave a positive impression:

Answer the question - Sounds simple, doesn't it? I've interviewed hundreds of potential candidates, and I am still shocked by how many people never answer the question that's been asked. When this happens, and it happens a lot, I'll typically ask a second time or press for the detail I'm looking for. If the candidate doesn't provide an answer the second time, their chance to join my team is quite low. This is especially true when this pattern continues throughout the interview.

Only answer the question - You should be able to answer just about any question in four to six sentences. If an answer is longer than that, you are quite likely talking too much. If there is additional important detail the interviewer(s) may want to hear, you can ask, "Would you like to hear more?" or "Is there additional detail you would like me to provide?" This gives the panel a chance to ask for more, or move on to the next question.

Follow the 80 / 20 rule - So how much should a candidate talk? If an interview is going well the interviewee will be talking about 20% of the time. That percentage may sound low, but think about it for a minute. Most interviews are scheduled for an hour. Introductions of the interview panel and small talk designed to make you more comfortable will last about 10 minutes. At some point, the interview lead will provide an overview of the company and the open opportunity you are being considered for. This will generally last about 10 minutes, and there will be 10 minutes at the end for you to ask a few questions. There are only 30 minutes left, or 50% of the time remaining! Given that an interviewer will almost always follow your response with commentary, there just isn't much candidate talking time built into a typical interview. If you are talking more than 30% of the time, there is a good chance the interview isn't going well. If you are talking 50% of the time or more, I can just about guarantee there won't be a second chance to respond to questions the panel didn't have time to ask. In most cases, the candidate who is talking a lot isn't doing well.

Use the right language - We like people who are similar to us, and that starts with using the same language and terms. Use this knowledge to your advantage! How can you learn the language of the company you want to join? It's easier than you might think. Start with reading all open job postings on the company website, being sure to jot down reoccurring themes and jargon. During the interview, use words from your research. Speaking the same language will help build a connection. It's important for the conversation to have a natural flow, so don't force an opportunity. This one can backfire, so proceed with caution.

Tie your skills to competencies important to the hiring company - When reading open position postings, you will learn what types of opportunities the hiring company is currently hiring for. Think strategically to gather insight into changes the company is going through or the direction they are headed. For example, look for a theme of "preferred competencies" in open job postings. If 'change management certification' or 'deep understanding of Lean principles' is frequently preferred, it would be wise to share examples of how your experience ties to these skills. This is true even if you have formal training in disciplines the company holds as important. Certification in desired disciplines is a bonus, even more impressive when you are able to articulate practical experience and results. Measurable experience will put you ahead of the competition.

Use mirroring techniques - Mirroring is simply adjusting your body language to match the person you are talking to. If they lean forward slightly, you do the same. Smile at your interviewer when they smile at you. This goes back to the idea that we like people who are similar to us. While mirroring is a very simple idea, using it in a natural way is something you'll want to work on. A little bit of practice on this technique will help to execute it naturally.

Don't fidget - It's distracting, and makes the interviewer wonder how well you will handle pressure. Leg shaking, hand wringing, ring twirling, and pen popping all make me want to say "Please relax, you're making me anxious", not the impression you want to leave behind.

Ask questions - About that 10 minutes reserved for you to ask questions, don't say "Well, you've already answered all of my questions"… really? You are considering spending a minimum of 40 hours a week with the people in this company for the next several years and there isn't a single thing you are curious about? The list of possible questions is endless so plan ahead to ask thoughtful questions. Think about what is important to you about company culture and processes. Here are few ideas to get you started on the path to asking a few insightful questions:

- How are accomplishments celebrated?
- What do the people interviewing you like best about working at the company?
- What research could you begin now in case you are the person selected of the position?
- What is it about this company that differentiates it from other employers?

Do a bit of Internet search for suggestions on interview questions. It's easy to find several great articles that will spark creative ideas. Find one or two you like in order to leave a positive last impression with thoughtful questions.

Thank you note - Send your interview team thank you notes the same day, or by end of the following day at the latest. There are divided camps on whether it's better to send an email, or a handwritten note through the mail. The handwritten note has a more personal touch; however, email is more efficient and interviewers will have a note waiting for them the next morning. Choose the method you prefer, just don't delay. Also, be on the lookout for too many "me" statements. Your note should be focused on the company and its customers, how you will add value as the selected candidate, and why your particular skills will fill a need on the team. This isn't the time to talk about your personal career goals. Lastly, send a separate note to each person on the interview panel, even if you decide to go with email. A group note looks lazy and lacks a personal touch.

Take deep breaths before an interview and remember you are the prize. An interview is equal parts you analyzing if this is a place you'll want to build a career, and the panel determining if your talents and approach fit the opportunity and company culture.

Lilly was the perfect addition to our family. Jeff and I spend a great deal of time with our two dogs and enjoy the closeness Vizslas' demand. Spend adequate time on the hiring process to make sure your next new hire is a fit for your work family.

Don't be dazzled by an impressive resume and flowery recommendations. Superb technical expertise won't bridge a culture gap or missing social skills necessary for success. Chances are high that the new hire will work for the organization for many years, so choices made in the hiring process impact every aspect of your organization. Be certain the selected candidate possesses the attitude, work ethic, and social skills needed to provide excellent service to customers and internal partners.

CHAPTER TWO

Networking

Lilly:

"I'm still learning how to meet people and leave them with a good impression of me. I know I'm not supposed to jump on my new friends, but it's just so hard to be calm!!! I have so much to tell my new friends, plus the anticipation of getting extra attention is almost more than a girl can stand!! My parents don't like it when I talk too much because it scares people, especially little kids. Sometimes I bark because I'm excited to meet new people. I have a lot to say and want my new friends to hear all about it!! I know my parents want me to sit quietly during the greeting, and I've noticed things go much better when I do. It's very hard because I have so much to tell people, especially the people that I REALLY want to meet.

There are so many ways to meet new people. I'm learning the best behaviors to get me the pets, treats, and sweet talk I want while leaving my new friends with a smile instead of a scowl. Mom calls this networking."

Training Lilly:

Learning how to have a positive experience when meeting new people is something Lilly struggled with for over a year. She just couldn't figure out how to get the attention she craved while creating a positive experience for her new human friends. Her inability to socialize caused several embarrassing situations. One of these events embedded in my memory occurred on a warm Arizona evening. It was a great night to take Jasalynn, my granddaughter, to the park near our home. The busy park was also the perfect place to work with Lilly on following commands when distractions were present. It was a beautiful idea!! What could go wrong?!?

Positioning Lilly about 40 feet away from the playground equipment seemed the perfect distance to work with her while keeping a close eye on Jasalynn. I was far enough away that Lilly was out of the reach of

27

the other kids, and I could get to my granddaughter quickly if she needed me. The element not included in the calculation was being far enough away from stupid parents. It is amazing how many people will let a small child approach a dog they don't know! On this visit there was a 4-year old girl at the playground who was absolutely determined to pet Lilly. She ran toward us several times waving her hands and screaming that she wanted to pet the dog. Lilly didn't react strongly at first, but she was clearly skittish and uncomfortable. Using a loud voice with the intention of getting the attention of the mother, I repeatedly asked the little girl to leave us alone because Lilly didn't know her. About 30 minutes into the training session, I was talking to Jasalynn and didn't notice the child running in our direction. As you can imagine, I was horrified when my sweet dog lunged and snapped her teeth. Now, to be fair... because I feel a maternal need to defend my dog... rushing and screaming in a high-pitched voice would get negative attention from most animals. Still, we couldn't allow Lilly to react that way. It was definitely time to include more socialization into her training routine.

Here's how we changed things to help Lilly learn a better way to respond to humans. Frequent trips were planned to PetSmart, dog parks, and dog friendly malls and restaurants. She went for long walks in the neighborhood almost every day and attended local art and craft fairs. Lilly is EXTREMELY treat driven, so bringing a few of her favorite snacks to show appreciation for good behavior was helpful. Rewarding Lilly with a treat when she sat quietly while people walked by or spoke to her went a long way to encouraging desired behaviors. The next step was to ask parents of older children, not the lunging screeching kind, for permission to ask the kid to help with a quick training session. The children were given treats and instructed to ask Lilly to sit. Lilly would be rewarded with a treat when she sat patiently while she was petted. The kids enjoyed helping out, and Lilly quickly learned how simple it was to get her reward. If she began to jump or show frustration, a gentle tug on the leash and letting her see the tasty treat was enough to get her back on track.

People decide if they can trust Lilly in about 15 seconds. Your first impression window isn't much longer. Learning to connect quickly and how to leave potential employers, colleagues, and networking connections with a positive impression are critical networking tools.

Lilly's Leadership Lesson:

First impressions follow us... if not forever, for a VERY long time! It only takes a few minutes (sometimes seconds) to create the lens an interviewer, new leader, or colleague will use to view everything you do and say. Even when we focus on objectivity and practice sincere listening, these judgments sneak in to reinforce first impressions.

We all have lenses for other people... and other people have lenses for us. Think about the last time you went to the optometrist for glasses or contacts. When the doctor was dialing in your new prescription, she tried several different options for vision correction. Keep the phrase "Better with one, or two... better with three, or four" in your mind. We do the same thing with people. There is a lens in the subconscious mind we see all interactions through. "Does Jane talk too much here, or here?... Is she listening poorly here, or here?". We see colleagues, friends, and family members through impression lenses we have prescribed for them.

We can use the tendency to view people through a lens to our advantage. Here are a few ways to influence the lens others will view you through:

Make a Connection

Life is all about connections. This is true in our personal lives and extends to the professional environment. Learning how to make connections improves our ability to expand professional circles at networking events and also enriches existing work relationships. Some people seem to be born with the natural ability to effortlessly connect quickly and effectively. The most successful people have turned networking into an art. So what is it that these well-connected people do that you can incorporate into your networking plan? Below is a list of behaviors that will help you make connections quickly, and strengthen existing relationships:

Use names - When you know someone's name, be sure to use it, and use it often. Natural points in a conversation to use a name are during the greeting and at the conclusion. Be deliberate about using names at these points, and create other opportunities where doing so flows with the conversation. Plugging a name into every other sentence will result in sounding like a used car salesman, quite opposite of the impression you are after! Addressing people by name is a quick way to form connections. People will remember you because you remember them.

Remind people of your name - Another name tip is to remind others of your name. Reintroduce yourself when you've only spoken a few times. This is especially helpful when speaking with busy executives or at networking events. It's as simple as extending your hand and saying, "Hi Sally, I'm Carla Howard. We meet last month at the strategic planning session". Just like that you've reintroduced yourself and avoided a potentially uncomfortable situation. Sally will remember you and your thoughtful approach long after the meeting.

Take notes - Jot down little details and save information where it can be quickly accessed. A few options for storing notes include Outlook, LinkedIn, Evernote, spiral notebooks (yes, they still exist!), or the use of a Word document on your computer. My personal favorite place to store networking notes is on LinkedIn. Using "tags" to group connections is a handy way to categorize contacts. Adding dozens of tags isn't helpful. Keep them high level and meaningful. The "relationship" tab in LinkedIn and the "How you met" field are other places to store details about the meeting and what was learned about the person. The type of information saved here should include the name of a spouse, a certification they are interested in, hobbies, or any other details that may be forgotten. These details help to engage in meaningful dialogue when meeting again. If you opt for the handwritten version, wait until the meeting is over to jot down your observations and thoughts.

Use positive language - Framing is a simple yet powerful tool. There is always a way to frame your thoughts in a positive and supportive way. A good indicator it may be time to change your framing language is when you hear yourself using limiting words and phrases like "have to", "no choice but to", "can't", or "always" followed by negative statements. Changing the message from "I need to leave early today, I have to be on a conference call at 9pm with Ankur from India", to "I'm leaving the office early today, I'll be speaking with Ankur from India at 9pm" puts a completely different spin on the activity. Better yet, end the statement with "I'm looking forward to speaking with Ankur from India tonight". You see the difference? In the first example the task sounds like drudgery, but in the later it's expected to be a positive experience.

Smile - Smiling makes people more approachable. We want to be around others who make us feel good.

If the day isn't going well, facial expressions shouldn't give that away. Colleagues are always watching how we carry ourselves and how we react to challenges and stress. If comments are often made about how busy or under stress you are, chances are good you aren't smiling enough.

Be Quiet - Now, don't take this one too far. You also don't want to answer every question with "yes", "no", or other one word responses. People who refuse to enter dialogue sound like petulant children. Make meaningful contributions to the discussion, but just be sure you aren't dominating the conversation. Ask open-ended questions to encourage others to do the talking. Look for opportunities to ask for additional detail to enhance your understanding of a topic.

Listen - I know, listening is on every list on how to be a great leader and in every book on the topic. It really is that important. Even the best listeners have room for improvement. When the brain is busy thinking about what we will do or say next, we aren't listening. Wondering if your boss answered that email you sent early this morning? You aren't listening. Not allowing the mind to wander is hard work! Truly focusing on the person you are talking to will improve every aspect of your life. I once had a leader who answered her phone every time it rang, even if we were in the middle of a conversation. She once answered her phone during my performance appraisal! Fight the urge to check your phone or watch, look at email, answer the phone, or any do anything else that shows you aren't invested in the conversation. Focusing on people is the only way to build connections and trust.

Remain Calm

When feeling anxious, frustrated, or afraid, it is particularly difficult to connect with people. These feelings may surface during formal networking events, interviews, or important meetings. Practicing the good habits below will help keep emotions in check:

Banish negative self-talk – This may be the most difficult habit to break. Negative self-talk sneaks in doors you didn't know were left open. When you hear that little voice in your head saying you don't belong, or that you don't have what it takes to be successful, boot it to the curb! Replacing negative running dialogue with positive messages has a profound impact on self-confidence and overall happiness. Listen closely; you may be surprised by what you hear. Anytime definitive thoughts such as "I always", "I never", "I can't", or "Every time <fill in the blank>", crosses your mind it's time to pay close attention to what comes next. Is what follows negative? If the answer is yes, stop and fill the space with emotional friendly language. Changing self-talk from "I don't mingle well at networking events" to "I'm learning how to meet new people" will put you in a better state of mind and decrease anxiety. Changing thought patterns is a big step toward moving away from being our worst critic toward becoming our biggest fan!

Watch your beverages - I don't mean hold on tightly so nobody steals them. The drinks you consume can have a negative impact on the ability to make a great first impression. One of these thirst quenchers could be the culprit:

- Caffeine - Coffee, soda, and energy drinks are often used to get the day started or provide an afternoon boost. They also raise adrenaline levels, which can put us in a state of nervousness. If you've ever experienced the jitters from too much caffeine, that anxious feeling that follows is familiar. The same adrenaline that causes shaky hands and a racing heart may contribute to a less than perfect reaction to a comment, email, or hallway discussion. When there is an important presentation or difficult situation looming at work, why add an accelerated heart rate to the equation? It's fine to enjoy that morning cup o' joe or afternoon pick-me-up in moderation. Be careful not to over indulge or reach for caffeinated drinks when a cool head is in order.

- Adult beverages - Yes, I'm talking about beer, wine, or your adult drink of choice. Use a bit of common sense here, and proceed with caution. There is nothing wrong with enjoying a glass of wine or a beer with colleagues. There is everything wrong with drinking to the point where you say or do something you wouldn't consider when sober. I've seen some pretty ugly behavior after one too many drinks at work functions, and I can only imagine the regret the next day. Even small slips of the tongue can cause embarrassment and tarnish an otherwise stellar reputation. The moderate drinking rule also applies to guests you bring to an event. I once attended a company Holiday party held at a posh local resort. The husband of one of my colleagues indulged in too much wine, and by the end of the evening he was attempting to kiss every woman in the room by dangling a piece of mistletoe he picked up from the dinner table centerpiece. I thought about the incident every time I saw my coworker who brought the kissing bandit, and I'm pretty sure I wasn't alone. The one drink rule would have likely kept that unfortunate event from happening and saved everyone from enduring an embarrassing situation.

Invoke the 80 / 20 Rule - People love to talk about themselves. Use that bit of knowledge to your advantage and be a great listener. Often people get anxious because they're afraid they won't have anything interesting to add to a conversation. Never fear! Most people will do darn near all of the talking if you let them. In fact, they will fill up close to 80% of the conversation. All you have to do is ask a few open-ended questions, and then listen. If they start to slow down and you don't have content to add, ask a question about something they've said. People will continue to talk about themselves for a very long time, especially when the listener has shown interest by asking follow-up questions. It's a good idea to have a few conversation starters prepared in case you need them, and being prepared will boost self-confidence. Using some variation of these questions is a good place to start:

- How did you get involved in <topic>?
- How do you think <topic> will change in the next 3 - 5 years?
- How long have you been a member of this association?
- What do you like best about being a <fill in profession title>?

Wear clothes you feel great in - We all feel better when we look our best. Go through your closet on a regular basis and discard items that are faded, show signs of wear, out of style, or don't fit properly. Don't forget to look closely at shoes when assessing what goes to Goodwill or the landfill. I find women are the worst offenders when it comes to wearing tired and worn out shoes. Ladies, if the heels of your pumps are marked up or the leather is cut, it is time to find a new favorite pair! One tip for keeping shoes looking great longer is to keep a pair of driving shoes in the car. Resting a heel on the floorboard is a sure fire way to ruin a shoe before its time. Remember, a professional wardrobe is a confidence booster and will improve the impression you leave behind. Plus, it's a great excuse to hit the sale rack to find that next great deal.

Networking Tips

Investing in building your network will pay huge dividends. In a typical week I dedicate 10 - 15 hours toward enriching and growing my personal circle. That may sound like a lot if you aren't actively dedicating time to this activity. The truth is, most of us have a few professional relationships that could use a bit of nurturing. Knowing there is time set aside every week for this purpose makes it part of the week versus something to add if time permits. Deliberate networking needs to be built into planned work. These social media sites and meeting tips should be part of that plan:

LinkedIn - I was skeptical of using LinkedIn in the beginning. Interviewing several colleagues who were active on the site proved to be persuading enough to give it a shot. The initial investment in creating a robust profile is the most time consuming activity. Those who have a current resume will find it easier to get started. Spend some time browsing the profiles of others for ideas on how to build an engaging profile. The most attractive sites tell professional stories well. Your brand is being built and defined by your profile along with every post, comment, like, share, and update. Activities that bring the most value Include:

- Build your network - Begin by connecting with current colleagues and previous co-workers. Remember to include friends and family into your online network. Once you have a few contacts, LinkedIn will help by recommending "people you may know". Make a mental note to send connection requests anytime new introductions have been made. Opportunities generally arise during these events:
  ☐ Training classes
  ☐ Project work

- ☐ Networking events
- ☐ Conferences
- ☐ Association chapter meetings
- ☐ Other gatherings of business professionals
- Use Hashtags (#) - Include a few (3 - 6) relevant hashtags to your posts. This simple strategy will increase traffic to your content, and boosts your visibility on the platform.
- ALWAYS personalize the invitation - It connects with people on a different level and makes the receiver feel like your interest is genuine.

Before you start sending those invitations, here are a few things to add to your "Don't Do" list. Never do these things:

- Send invitations to people you don't know. Most people won't accept invitations from professionals they haven't met anyway. There is one exception to this advice. When searching for a different job it can be helpful to reach out to several recruiters. Limit your connection requests to people you've met unless there is a valid business reason to reach out. Including a brief description in the invitation gives it a personal touch. People are suspicious of the motive behind requests from strangers; so a little bit of detail will help to calm their concerns.

- Connect too soon with people inside the company you work for. Wait until you've had more than a five-minute discussion to reach out. Invitations are more natural to receive after several conversations or working on a joint project.
- Use it as a dating site. Yes, it happens… and it's infuriating, creepy, unprofessional, and off-putting.
- Fail to upload a photo. A picture will help find you. LinkedIn users want to be certain they are connecting with the right person. Even though LinkedIn is a professional site, it is social media. A picture helps make your profile more approachable and your content (updates, likes, shares, etc.) easier to associate with you.

Post a professional picture. A great photo will help to build your brand, and a poorly selected shot does the opposite. I see picture mistakes every time I open LinkedIn. Browsing the site will provide several examples of these mistakes:

- Selfies - Never post a selfie: just don't do it. Save that digital self-portrait for Facebook, Instagram and other personal sites.

- Family pictures - LinkedIn is about YOU. Use that family shot on the beach for next years' Christmas card, not your professional profile.
- Vacation photos - LinkedIn isn't show and tell. Under no circumstances should a profile shot be taken in front of the coliseum in Rome, on the ski slopes, or with a gigantic fish. Nobody (and I mean NOBODY) needs to see you wearing a sleeveless shirt paired with sandals and shorts on the beach. Is that really the image you want to project?
- Animals - The "hiking with my dogs" photo is good for the desk, not LinkedIn.
- Exercise shots - Not a personal trainer? ... We don't want to see it. In fact, even if you are a professional trainer it is better to get out of those sweaty workout clothes before getting a photo snapped.
- Cropping people out of the picture - We can still see them!! That hand on your shoulder is a dead giveaway.
- Obvious home / office background – Take a spin through LinkedIn and see how many ridiculous backdrops you can find. I went on a quick tour while writing this chapter and within 5 minutes found these terrible backdrops:
  - ☐ In a home kitchen - Without even bothering to clean up the counter!
  - ☐ Hallways – The mirrors and pictures on the walls make the hall easy to spot.

- ☐ In front of a window - Blinds open or closed, it doesn't work either way.
- ☐ Hiking - On the trail, at the top of a mountain, or any scenic spot along the way. Just say no.
- ☐ In a car - That expensive ride probably isn't yours anyway. If it is, bragging isn't attractive on anyone.
- ☐ Swimming pool - Even if you're fully clothed it's a bad idea.
- Pictures that don't include YOU - That scenic shot of a sunrise, valley, or beach won't help people find you.
- Holding an instrument - Of course, band members and instrument repair shops get a pass on this one. Otherwise, change your career or your picture.
- Trying to be cool - Wearing sunglasses, ball caps, stocking caps, sports jerseys, or throwing us a peace sign, high-five, or thumbs up… it's not cool.
- Holding a wine glass or beer - Seriously?!?!? Yes, there are actually pictures out there of people drinking alcohol. If this is you and you don't own a winery or craft beer microbrewery, do yourself a favor and stop reading this book long enough to remove your profile picture.

You get the picture, keep it classy. It's that simple.

Facebook - This social site is a great way to keep

track of family and friends. It's not great for colleagues:

- Keep Facebook personal. Colleagues and your professional network don't need to know intimate details about the weekend or what friends and family are up to. I suspect we all have at least one relative or friend who posts things you wouldn't want to be associated with at work. Remember, every comment and "like" selected is visible to your Facebook network. For better or worse, anything associated with you will impact your personal brand. This is a very strict rule for me, LinkedIn is for professional networking and Facebook is for my children and close friends, no exceptions.
- Make sure your page is private. Then check again. The percentage of public accounts is somewhere between the 20% - 30% range; make sure yours isn't one of them. We've all heard stories about people who post updates that put them in uncomfortable positions or cause employment termination. Just for fun, check to see how many colleagues you can find with public profiles. Some of the posts may surprise you. I've seen posts that range from tirades about their jobs and bosses, to silly updates like "Bored a work, I guess it's time to check out the candy dishes!" Avoid embarrassing situations by being thoughtful about what you share online.

• Only post what you wouldn't mind a boss or potential employer seeing, even when your page is private. The pictures and comments on your page are visible to a much wider audience when connections "like" or share your posts. Also, site settings aren't foolproof. Websites may change rules, guidelines, and security options that will allow access to unintended viewers. There is also the possibility of glitches on the site, or someone copying and pasting your update and making it visible via reposting, emails, blogs, etc. To be safe, don't post pictures or information that could compromise your integrity.

Twitter - Enhancing your personal brand with posts containing no more than 140 characters can be challenging. If you've stayed away from Twitter, I'd encourage you to give it a try. Many professional tweets contain links to articles, quotes, pictures, and the occasional personal message or thought.

• Start off by following a few people with similar interests. Enter keywords in the search bar (then enter) and Twitter will display articles and posts containing that word. There are also several articles on the internet that include lists of interesting people to follow. You can find these lists by searching with phrases like "Who to follow on Twitter" or "Women to follow on Twitter".

- Make it easy for potential followers to find you by using your name in either your profile or user name.

- Create a professional description to let potential followers know what type of tweets they can expect.

- Decide how you want to be perceived, and be deliberate in your postings. If leadership is a strong element of your brand, tweet links to related articles, quotes, and thoughts on the topic. It's a good idea on this site to post personal content on occasion. This is much different from LinkedIn where personal posting is frowned upon. Adding a personal touch will help connect with followers. Just remember, you are building your brand with every tweet... so keep it classy!

- Use hashtags. Don't go overboard. There are only 140 characters available, so use the space wisely. Also, there is no need to add a hashtag to every tweet. I typically will add one at the front of words associated with my brand.

- Be social. It's important to interface with followers and those you follow. Share tweets from others and always give credit by placing @username in front of your tweet. Interact with your followers and be generous with comments, likes, and replies.

47

Instagram - This forum is my guilty pleasure. I adore Instagram! It's easy and filled with fascinating pictures. Descriptions are usually short or nonexistent. This makes it easy to view several pictures during a quick break in my busy day. You can set up either a personal or a professional account, but choose one option and stick with it. One word of caution: only post pictures you wouldn't mind people at work seeing, because they will! To be successful on Instagram, the guidelines are similar to those for Twitter. Use hashtags, be social, use a profile to describe the type of pictures people can expect to see, and have fun!

Even with all of our electronic forms of communication and the rise of social media, nothing replaces meeting in person. Even a quick two-minute discussion forms a tighter bond than an email. When planning a networking strategy, build in intentional face-to-face conversations. These interactions are the best tools for strengthening your network and building strong relationships. Here are a few ways to add extra conversation time into the week:

Town Halls and other large company meetings

- Don't sit with your team or others you work with on a regular basis! Use this opportunity to spend time with people you don't know very well. Better yet, find a section of the room where you don't know anyone and introduce yourself.
- Did someone receive an award or other recognition during the event? If so, congratulate them! This is great time to shake hands and make an introduction if the award winner is a colleague you haven't worked with.

Breakfast meetings - Early morning is a great time to connect with people. We've all been in conversations where someone will say, "Let's get together for lunch, we really need to catch up!"… and it just never happens. Mornings are my secret weapon. This time of day is much easier to schedule and will rarely be double booked.

- Whom should you schedule breakfast with? I generally use mornings to connect with previous colleagues, new acquaintances I've met through networking events, and current colleagues for non-work related discussions. An occasional coffee with friends during the week does happen, but this time is generally reserved to grow my professional network.

- Morning coffee doesn't interfere with work. It's a time you can spend visiting without being seen as an office social butterfly.
- Do favors in the morning. Not everyone is a morning person, but most people will be glad to get up early to meet when you're doing them a favor. For example, I do quite a bit of coaching on change management, and I mentor several women professionals. While coaching and leading change are part of my day job, 6:30am - 8:00am is reserved to help people in my extended network. People will generally be more than willing to wake up an hour early when they know you are volunteering personal time.
- It's easy to stay on time. Restaurants and coffee shops aren't extremely busy super early so service is typically quick. Additionally, you both need to leave in time to start your workday so meetings don't linger.

Lunch - I realize I'm probably in the minority here, but I'm not a fan of lunch meetings. In fact, I rarely schedule more than one or two lunch meetings per month. Here's why:

- Meetings in the office can run late making it difficult to arrive back to work on time.
- Last minute cancellations are common. It feels terrible to be the one to cancel, and it can be

frustrating on the receiving end of a request to reschedule.

- Lunch is significantly more expensive than a cup of coffee. For those who schedule a few networking meetings each week, the tab can add up very quickly. A lower price option is more considerate toward the person you are meeting as well. Even the most budget conscious colleagues can typically squeeze the cost of coffee into a weekly budget.

When lunch is the only option, here are a few ways to make it work:

- Reserve this time for colleagues within your current company who you work with on a daily basis. The ability to see calendars will make it easier to schedule a convenient time for both of parties. When business conflicts make it necessary to cancel, the reasons are generally well known or easily explained.
- Make the meeting short. When your lunch partner is down the hallway, it's convenient to meet in the cafeteria or lunchroom. Often, it's possible to cut the time to 30 minutes when business issues arise.
- Don't forget BYOL (Bring your own lunch) - It's much less expensive and is often a healthier option.

Send thank you cards - I'm a big fan of handwritten thank you cards. It feels great when a bright envelope arrives in the mail or sits propped on your keyboard with a sincere note of thanks on the inside. Send cards when the assistance and / or time commitment was significantly outside of normal job responsibilities. Thank you cards are also a nice touch when a new connection takes time out of the day to meet.

Email your gratitude - This is the best choice for smaller appreciation messages, or when it's important the note is received quickly. Send generously as they reinforce positive behaviors and build relationships at the same time.

Reintroduce yourself - When in situations where you aren't certain if the other person will remember a past meeting, extend your hand and saying, "Hi Joe, I'm John Setter. We met at the better speaking luncheon last December" It's especially helpful when the initial introduction was several months ago, or if the two of you have only spoken a few times. The reintroduction also removes pressure for John to remember your name and where you met. Additionally, John will leave the conversation thinking of you as a polished professional.

Help others become successful - You have expertise that can add value to your network. Freely share your knowledge and skills, using them to help others be successful. It feels great, and people will remember that you took time to help them. The more we focus on others, the more successful and fulfilled our careers become. Here are a few ways to share expertise and stay connected:

- Coaching - Serving as a mentor or coach improves leadership skills and forges strong relationships. Sharing expertise helps people achieve success in ways that wouldn't have been possible without your contribution. When our hearts are open to serving others, we learn and grow in the process of helping them achieve their goals. Sometimes all the person needs is a few minutes to talk through a sticky situation. Whether the request for coaching comes through casual conversations, speaking engagements, project assignments, or other activities, try to find a way to say yes to mentoring. You'll be glad you did!

- How to say yes, by saying no - Sometimes we simply don't have the skill or time to do what someone is asking of us. In those moments, here are a few ways to be of service without saying yes to the task. Ask a few clarifying questions to understand the underlying need.

Many times people will ask for a specific action or favor when there are different, often better ways to solve the problem. Here is an example of what I'm talking about. My daughter, Bailey, took a very difficult college math course last semester. She was struggling in class and asked if I would help her with a particularly difficult homework assignment. I spent all day one frustrating Saturday looking at her math problems, and researching math concepts online that I hadn't used in a very long time. At the end of a six-hour study stint, I called my mom, exhausted and frustrated. When she learned how I was spending my "day of rest", mom recommended that I ask a college student who lived on her street if he would tutor Bailey. Instead of racking my brain and spending the rest of my weekend in math purgatory, I paid the neighbor kid $20 an hour to help my daughter. Problem solved! What Bailey really needed was help with her homework, who did the helping wasn't important. So…

- Define the end goal. What actually needs to be accomplished? Are there other ways to meet the need?
- Say yes to a smaller part of the request. If someone were to ask me to train his or her dog, I could share how we trained Lilly.

- If you don't have the skill to complete the task, help them find others who do.
- Get professional help. The proverb, "If money can fix a problem, then it really isn't a problem" is true. Direct people to contract resources who can meet their needs.

Lilly is a people magnet. Her breed is uncommon, she's a beautiful dog (I might be a little biased), and the fact that she is generally well behaved garners her a lot of attention. Strangers want to get to know Lilly when she sits patiently and waits for them to approach. When our gal is jumping and licking unsuspecting "new friends" like an ice cream cone on a hot day, the results are quite different! Lilly is learning which behaviors lead to positive attention, an occasional treat, and more outings with mom and dad.

Networking doesn't come natural to most of us. It's a skill, and like all skills, we improve with practice. Many times it's the people who believe they have mastered the art of connecting that have the most to learn. Casual conversations are great; however, nothing replaces making and maintaining connections with a focused and deliberate approach. Spend dedicated time each week building relationships and expanding your network. It will enhance your career, and you just might find your personal life enriched in the process.

CHAPTER THREE

Training

Lilly:

"I started puppy class at ten weeks old. For almost a year, my parents took me to training every weekend to work with our trainer Mariah. I loved it because I received loads of attention and a new toy after almost every class! I've graduated from puppy, intermediate, and advanced training. Pretty soon I'll be ready to take my Canine Good Citizen test. At the beginning of each training session, we show Mariah how good I am at doing the tricks and behaviors taught during the prior weeks' lesson. Next, we learn a few new things to practice until our next class. I learn two or three new commands and at least one fun trick at each session. I like going to training most of the time, but I get frustrated during practice. Some of the commands are hard, and I don't always understand what I'm supposed to do. I've done the basic commands so many times that I am excellent at them. That's because I completely understand exactly what I'm supposed to do, and I get them right every time!! A few examples of things I'm good at are "sit", "down", "wait", and "go to your bed". We've just started working on how to play hide and seek. I really like that game and I'm getting better very quickly! My parents spend more time than I'd like on heeling. I don't like to heel, but that doesn't stop my parents from making me do it! I know I have a lot to learn, but I just can't learn it all at once. I perform much better with shorter practice sessions that have play and fun included.

I enjoy learning, especially when the training is delivered in the way I like to learn and within time intervals that match my attention span."

Training Lilly:

Lilly isn't my first dog. As far back as I can remember, my family has included at least one member from the canine group. All of our dogs have been fairly well behaved and able to perform basic commands. When we brought Lilly home, my husband and I decided we wanted a more highly trained companion this time around. Lilly's first training class started when she was 10 weeks old, and we plan to continue with formal training for about two years. We want Lilly to join us on vacations, dinner out to dog friendly restaurants, and we're considering training her to be a therapy dog for children. All of these situations require Lilly to be well behaved and able to understand a wide variety of commands. I suppose we could have approached obedience training by reading books on how to train your puppy, watching a few videos, and asking friends for advice. Although these have been great supplements, we decided formal training was the best way to go.

We've invested heavily in training process, and I'm not just talking about the cost of training, treats, and the other supplies good dog parents own. All of our training classes are scheduled on Sundays, which means weekends are planned around training Lilly. Then there is homework, which includes focused work on commands and consistently correcting her behavior during the day. Going to obedience classes taught us how to train Lilly, but practice has been the key to making positive behavior changes and in her ability to perform a wide variety of commands.

We quickly learned there is a cap on the length of

time Lilly can practice for sessions to be effective. As she gets older and gains proficiency, her capacity for longer and more intense bouts of training increases. At 8 - 20 weeks practice only lasted about 10 - 15 minutes. During those weeks we worked with her in short bursts 3 - 6 times a day. Once she was proficient in the basics and a few weeks older, training sessions extended to 15 - 20 minutes and continued to increase gradually. Now we can incorporate training and play (when training is fun, Lilly doesn't know the difference) and practice sessions can last two hours or more. As Lilly's skill and proficiency increase, her behavior, confidence, and attitude do too. Taking Lilly to training was essential, but training didn't create a well-mannered dog. If that were the case there would be fewer pups in adoption shelters and training prices would be extreme. Patience, along with many hours of practice, was necessary to instill positive behaviors and competence in executing commands.

People need training when they are expected to make a change in the way they work, but training alone won't achieve desired results. Knowing what to do before and after training improves the experience for employees as well as the business outcomes.

Lilly's Leadership Lesson:

Training doesn't change behaviors or create proficiency. Logically this makes sense, yet how many times is "send them to training" the first thing we jump to when attempting to initiate change? While training is an important part of any transition, there are important steps before and after training we shouldn't skip over. When the primary focus is on skill instruction, results are disappointing to say the least. The amount of practice and coaching needed is determined by a persons' learning capacity, natural ability for the subject matter, and the level of difficulty of the task. Since these are different for everyone, it's a leaders' job to analyze the best path to success for each employee.

Brilliant leaders are thoughtful about what needs to happen before training, the type of instruction employees need, and how much practice each person needs to be proficient.

Before Training

Have you ever sat in a training class or business meeting, and instead of hearing the message, you hear something like "Charlie Brown teacher voice"? I have, and I suspect you're nodding your head in agreement. When thoughts are focused on tasks waiting at the desk or errands waiting for us after work, we're not focused on learning how to use a new software system. Most of us attend training with the intent to be good learners, but our ability to focus is severely diminished when basic information is missing.

Transitions are difficult. It's not easy to change, and let's face it… we only attend training when we want to change something in our lives, or we have been asked to do so by others. The subject of the change may be more of a personal competency, such as learning to listen more keenly or how to hold difficult conversations, or it may involve learning new technical skills. Either way, the desired end result is a change. If we don't demonstrate the desired outcome, training isn't effective and our money and time have been wasted.

There are a few simple steps to take before your employees are scheduled for training in order to lay the foundation for a successful experience. Here's how to banish the Charlie Brown teacher experience:

- Tie the reason for training to the vision and strategy of the company. Better yet, engage your executive team in delivering this message. People perform better when they understand why a change is being implemented, and they like to hear strategic messages from high-level leaders. As a bonus, getting senior leaders to communicate more frequently raises their competency in leading change and greatly improves the likelihood that the initiative will be successful. Everyone wins!

- Provide details on how work will change in the future, why this particular training is necessary, and how new skills will help the employee achieve high levels of success in the future. Be as specific as possible and listen closely for concerns or objections. If you've ever sat in a training class or process improvement workshop wondering why you were there, you've had first-hand experience on why it's dangerous to skip this step.

- Tell people what will remain the same. There is a great deal of comfort in knowing what won't change. Sending clear messages on what will remain the same reduces resistance and anxiety. This is a critical tactic when ambiguity in the future state exists. Knowing what will remain constant, even if unrelated to the change, will bring stability and a sense of calm to the organization.

- Have a "heart to heart" conversation. Talk with direct reports about benefits to them personally when they become proficient in the new skills. As their leader, you know your employees better than anyone else does. Build the bridge of understanding between learning the new skill to job satisfaction and personal gain.

- Share what is at risk if new skills aren't learned and implemented. This may include what's at risk for the individual, customers, and the company. Provide as much detail as possible and explain consequences of not participating fully. Learning is a choice, and it only happens when people decide to engage in the change. This is a helpful tactic when employees are feeling reluctant or uninterested in the change.

Training is expensive, and not just in terms of costs related to creating workshops, job aids, and salaries during sessions. The steps and costs associated with improving processes and tools are also quite costly. When employees are not adept in the new way of working, results are disappointing and expected return on investment will not be achieved. Be thoughtful on how you will prepare employees for successful training experiences.

Developing Training

Does everyone who you expect to do something different need to be trained? The short answer is "Yes". That may sound unrealistic, especially if you are responsible for implementing transitional change spanning a large organization; however, it's much more realistic than rolling out changes and expecting everyone to adapt without instruction. Every time we expect people to work differently some level of training is necessary, but that doesn't mean training has to be a burden. On the contrary, the right level of instruction is a relief. While the topic of training is far too broad to cover in this short chapter, below you'll find tips to consider anytime you need people to execute work differently. These apply whether the desired change is related to work processes or behaviors and competencies:

Clearly define future state - To create the proper training program, it's necessary to paint a picture of what the future state will look like. This includes processes and tools, organization structure, and competencies each employee group will need to be successful.

Identify employee groups - Create a list of all groups who will need to perform their jobs differently in the future state. Bubble them up into groups that are impacted similarly. Don't leave anyone out. If you find yourself thinking, "Well, the finance team will only experience a very small change so I'll leave them off the list", stop right there. The finance team does need to be included as one of your employee groups. This groups' training will likely be simple. In fact, you may find a 10-minute discussion is all the training they will need.

Conduct a skills assessment - There are many assessment tools available for this step. A quick Internet search will uncover several to choose from or you can create your own. Start with each of your employee groups. List the skills and knowledge they need to be successful in the future state, and compare that list to their current skills and knowledge. Next, develop training plans to improve skills in the gap between current and future needs. This can be a time consuming portion of planning the curriculum; however, doing a thorough job in the planning phase greatly improves the training product.

Consider learning styles - There are dozens of different ways to provide training and instruction. Understand unique learning preferences and special challenges of the different learning groups. This will help to select the best method.

Before sending employees to training, do a bit of investigation to make sure the selected workshop will meet their needs, and the content is right for what you are trying to achieve. As you develop training plans for direct reports, take these steps to create strong development plans.

Apply Training

Sitting in a classroom seat to learn new skills doesn't add value to a team or the organization. Only when learned skills and techniques are applied to daily work will ROI (Return on Investment) be achieved. Be deliberate in following up with employees to ensure practicing what they've learned is built into their day. Support them by showing interest, providing coaching, and letting them know that you understand practice is part of gaining proficiency.

When you're the learner, it's time to practice what you preach. Find time to work on new skills and let your team know how you are doing along the way. People watch leaders and take cues on acceptable behavior, so show them investing in practice is important and expected after attending training. Be sure to keep your manager informed along the training journey. This will accomplish two things:

- First, your manager will be pleased to know it was worth the investment and that you are focused on adding value to the business.
- Second, demonstrating use of what you learned in a tangible way will increase the odds of

getting approval for the next cool development opportunity.

Few things are more frustrating than spending time and money to send people to training to have nothing change as a result. Encourage your team to openly share the changes they make, and be transparent in sharing how you apply new concepts and skills. Some changes may be very small, but the fact that changes were made is huge. Here's an example:

Several years ago, our team attended an excellent facilitation skills workshop. Some of the techniques taught during the day were creative ways to segment large groups into smaller breakout teams. One of these methods was to place four different types of small candy on a plate. Each person had to pick one. They could eat the candy but had to save the wrapper. There were just enough candies for each person to select one. We formed teams by grouping people based on the type of candy they selected. It was a fun and different from anything we had done in the past. Several months later, my boss and I were creating the choreography for a workshop, and I recommended we split up teams using the candy method. The participants in the workshop had fun with the exercise, and my boss had validation that sending me to training was worth the investment. Demonstrating ROI is as important for individuals as it is for teams and organizations.

Ability isn't instant

People aren't able to perform just because they've attended a training workshop, received instruction on how to use a system, or new processes have been explained. We all need a bit of time to practice new skills, and some of us will need a lot of practice! Brilliant leaders know their employees better than anyone else in the workplace. Employees are counting on their direct leader to create an environment where training, coaching, and time to practice is built into the plan. Great leaders consider unique needs for each of their employees and make sure the right training and coaching plans are in place for everyone to make a successful transition. These leaders create a framework for practice and plans for proficiency.

How many times have you seen practice built into a project plan? My guess would be not often enough. Sure, the project team will test the system and run mock scenarios to make sure transactions are running as expected. That's not the type of practice I'm talking about. Every employee who needs to work differently to realize project objectives will need time to practice.

Here are a few ways thoughtful practice can be incorporated during times of change:

Facilitate Training workshops - This is likely the most obvious option, and a necessary step for changes that significantly change the way work is performed. There is a tendency to deploy a "one size fits all" approach to training. Resist the urge to pack information and content for every employee group into a single workshop, and challenge any program that includes instruction on activities or processes your team doesn't need to learn. Analyze what is changing for each employee group, then create training specific to what they need to know. Throwing in extra content to cover more groups in a single sitting is frustrating for everyone involved.

Create Job aids - Step-by-Step job aids work well for simple changes or as a supplement to training workshops. Language should be simple and easy to follow. Screen shots need to be current, which means job aids need to be revised when systems are upgraded. When mentioning roles, use titles instead of employee names. Nothing will date your job aids more quickly than the name of a person who has left the company or moved on to a different role. To test the ease of use, ask someone not involved in creating the document to follow instructions to complete a task. If it's confusing to them, it will be confusing to others as well.

Produce Video's and Voice-over-PowerPoint - Create instructional videos using PowerPoint, Video, or screen trackers so people can see the system navigation. These should be quick (no more than 8 minutes) and cover a specific topic. Create multiple segments to keep modules short.

Implement a "Coach on Call" program – Formalize who will provide coaching and create an easy to use support plan. This is especially true when the new behavior or process is highly disruptive to the way work is performed. Knowing coaches are available will reduce the anxiety that comes with learning to be proficient. An example of when I've seen this done well was during implementation of a new WMS (Work Management System) in a warehouse environment. About six weeks prior to go-live, people who would serve as coaches at implementation and the two months that followed began wearing red smocks instead of the standard blue smocks. This made it easy for people on the warehouse floor to find help, and recognized SME's (subject matter experts) for their role on the project.

Set-up onsite help stations - Real-time, easy to access help is critical when implementing complex change. These temporary stations should be located directly on the shop floor or in the impacted office, and staffed with knowledgeable professionals. I've found help stations to be particularly useful when new technology is introduced to a work group. Ideally, technical support will be immediate and support is given without the requirement of opening problem tickets. These help desk stations are temporary, generally lasting only one or two weeks post implementation. After help stations are disbanded, employees will seek assistance in accordance with normal work procedures.

Create a Hot Line - This dedicated phone line only handles calls related to a specific change. It should be in place at go-live and remain active anywhere from a few days to a few weeks. The ideal length of timeframe for the hot line depending on these factors:

- Complexity of the change
- Number of people expected to perform work differently
- Risk to customer deliveries and satisfaction
- Identification of issues requiring immediate resolution

Dedicated inbox - Provide a dedicated inbox for employees, and in some situations customers and suppliers, to ask questions or raise concerns around the change. Develop automated messages to let senders know when they should expect a reply. Set up standard procedures and assign an owner to the process to ensure the stated response times are met. Create the dedicated inbox when a major change is announced and keep it operational for several weeks post implementation. The number of requests will diminish as people gain proficiency in the new process. This is a good indicator it's time to deactivate the inbox.

Suspend Metrics - Suspending performance metrics for a set period of time can go a long way toward lessening the stress of becoming proficient during change. This is particularly true when metrics are tied to incentive pay or a bonus plan. This works well when leaders temporarily suspend metric for one quarter, and apply the previous quarters metric to calculate financial incentives. When employees know they aren't expected to be perfect immediately, and management has built in time for them to gain proficiency without negative consequences during the learning process, two great things happen. First, stress levels are lowered and the change is less disruptive. Second, trust in the leadership team rises significantly.

Augment Staff - No business can allow customer service to suffer while employees gain ability. Lower levels of proficiency result in fewer products shipped, fewer responses to inquiries, slower service delivery, and additional checks to maintain quality. To meet customer demand and expectation, it may be necessary to add temporary employees to your team. Typically, additional help will come in the form of contract labor. Hire supplemental help before the additional support is needed. Build in the necessary time for training, and yes… include time for contractors to practice. It's a big mistake to hire in supplemental help a week before a big change or waiting until service levels have dropped. It's important for contractors to attain high levels of proficiency so they are able to help when the team needs them most. Set clear expectations on how long the engagement will last, and share your plan openly with temporary and permanent employees.

Conduct Parallel Processing - This is a form of UAT (user acceptance testing) on steroids. Run actual scenarios through new processes and systems several weeks prior to go-live. Include the "happy path" or perfect scenarios, as well as difficult situations the team has experienced. When possible, simulate true work volume and then increase volume and velocity to check performance under stress. If it's not possible to conduct parallel processing during the regular hours, consider running testing in the evenings or over weekends when customers won't be impacted. Although it's time consuming, this form of testing provides critical information to the project team, and begins building proficiency as employees learn how to use new systems and processes.

Listening Posts - Make it easy for your direct reports to share feedback on the effectiveness of training and what they need from you and their peers to make successful transitions. A few ways to incorporate listening posts are ballot boxes dedicated to collecting feedback, creating lunches with leaders where concerns and successes are openly shared, one-on-one conversations, and engaging in MBWA (management by walking around).

Remember, everyone needs time to practice after training to gain ability to meet customer and team expectations. Ability isn't automatic. Employees make successful transitions when leaders understand the importance of including a plan for practice after training.

Good leaders find the right training to teach skills employees need to be successful. Brilliant leaders build in time to practice and provide coaching during the transition.

Finding the right obedience program for Lilly was an important step in her training journey; however, one hour a week with Mariah didn't create a well-behaved companion. Over the past year, we've spent 10 - 20 hours each week on commands and teaching her the boundaries for life in our family. Some of the lessons come quite easily to our gal, others are still a work in progress.

CHAPTER FOUR

Recognition and Rewards

Lilly:

"I'll do just about anything for a delicious piece of chicken jerky or a peanut butter treat!!! Sometimes I have a hard time learning new things, but when my mom and dad have one of my favorite snacks in their hands I'll work hard until I get it right. I also like it when my mom says, "Thank you, Lilly",... and she says it a lot. That must be because I am such a good girl. When we go for walks and I leave sticks on the sidewalk instead of picking them up (which is SUPER hard to do) she thanks me and gives me a nice pat on the head. Sometimes people look at us strangely. They think I'm just a dog (I hate that saying) and that I don't understand, but I do. I'm doing my best to please my parents and when they thank me, pat me on the head, or take a few seconds during a walk to give me a good belly rub I feel great! It puts a little pep in my step, and I'm sure it shows. It feels good to perform well for people who appreciate me. I'm very happy to part of this family. I wouldn't want to live anyplace else.

I also get attention when I'm not behaving well, but I don't like it. A little bit of praise and an occasional treat is all it takes to encourage me to work hard."

Training Lilly:

Lilly is one of the most treat driven dogs I've ever known. Now, I know what you're thinking… all dogs love treats!! This is certainly true; however, it seems that Lilly takes her love of treats to a completely different level. This is an advantage when teaching her new behaviors and tricks, but it was also a disadvantage when we started transitioning to getting the same level of performance without dangling a treat in front of her nose. The good news is that she also responds well to praise, attention, and a simple but genuine "Thank you, Lilly". Yep, we actually say, "Thank you, Lilly" when she is performing well. You might think that sounds a bit silly, but it works for her. Lilly knows "Thank you" means she is doing a good job, and it encourages her to continue listening and doing what we ask. This is especially helpful when she is healing or performing other difficult commands and her attention starts to wander.. When we thank Lilly, she looks up and prances a bit. Praise is clearly a boost to her self-esteem!

Of course, we also have to let Lilly know when she is misbehaving. We have a specific voice command to let her know we aren't pleased. Lilly always hears this reminder when she jumps on fellow walkers, takes dishtowels off the counter, or barks at people on the street. While both positive and negative reinforcement are necessary, she responds more quickly to praise than punishment. When we focus on what Lilly is doing well, her manners quickly improve, and we have more fun in the process.

Finding what motivates Lilly was an important first step in her training journey. Uncovering what motivates your employees will help you be a better leader during times of change and provide positive ways to reinforce behaviors that bring the most value to your team and organization. It works for Lilly, and it will do the same for people in your life.

Lilly's Leadership Lesson:

It feels good be recognized for good work that adds value to our customers, colleagues, and the company we work for. Recognition is incredibly important in leading teams, coaching individuals, and managing change. Unfortunately, this reinforcement tool is often relegated to a task, overlooked, or purposely ignored. In the worst cases, the only reinforcement is negative consequences when things don't go according to plan.

Budget is a topic that almost always comes up when conversation turns to recognition and rewards. More precisely, funds often haven't been allocated for celebrating success. Many leaders and project managers believe they aren't able to reward employees without a large budget earmarked for recognition. Let's be honest, do you know anyone who has an unlimited budget or a large fund set aside for recognition? I doubt it, but that doesn't mean we can't find meaningful ways to show gratitude. Big celebrations and monetary incentives aren't the only way to recognize great work. Here are few ideas to consider that cost very little, and will leave a lasting impression:

Simply say "Thank you", or "Congratulations"

Do you say thank you enough at work? Most of us don't. Not because we aren't appreciative, our days are just so darn busy. It can be difficult to slow down long enough to think about the great work people are doing for us. I'm not suggesting that you "find" something to be grateful for. That would come across as contrived and insincere. People are doing great work all around us, thanking them shows you've noticed. It also builds self-esteem, and lets colleagues know what you'd like them to do more of.

Saying "Thank you" is the simplest, and often the most effective form of recognition. Telling someone you appreciate their work, or that you are proud of their accomplishments goes a long way toward reinforcing desired behaviors. I have a personal example I share every time I'm met with the "no budget" excuse for not creating meaningful rewards plans.

First, it's important to know a bit of the backstory. I was in my 40's when I decided it was time to return to college to complete my bachelor's degree. For a few years, I was on the full-time work / part-time college plan. The final two years I was a full-time student in the evening and worked full-time during the day. At the beginning of this crazy hectic schedule, I accepted a global role in a new company. I was in learning overload!!! With a lot of support from my husband and family, I found a way to make it work, so in May 2013 I graduated with a B.S. in General Business, with a minor in Management. Two weeks prior to graduation, my husband came in from checking the mail and handed me an envelope from my employer. I suspected it was an HR promotion about benefits, 401K status, or perhaps a brochure encouraging employees to walk 10K steps each day (our company was running a healthy steps initiative at the time). I remember being very tired and not in the mood deal with it, so I let the envelope sit on my desk until the next day. When I opened it, I found a handwritten note from a Sr. Executive I worked with on a regular basis. He sent the note to congratulate me on my graduation. A HANDWRITTEN note.... delivered to my house.... recognizing a significant personal achievement. Wow!! Today, three years later, I can recite that note word-for-word, yet I couldn't tell you the amount of my last bonus check. That note was recognition that mattered to me. It was personal and specific, and the only cost was a stamp and ten minutes of this executives' time.

We ask a lot of employees and colleagues. Take a few seconds to send a note that says "Perfect! This is just what I was looking for" is a quick and easy way to show appreciation. Here are a few things to remember about thank you notes.

Be timely - Don't delay! Tell people how much their work means to you as soon as the job is done.

Put leaders on copy - Copy the direct leader of the person you are acknowledging on your email. If the effort or results were extraordinary, consider including senior leaders. A good time to copy leaders two or three levels up are when the contribution was key to achieving a strategic goal, required an immense time commitment, or extended far outside of the employee's traditional role.

Keep cards handy - Buy a set of thank you cards, and make them visible on your desk as a reminder to send often. Better yet, give everyone on your team a supply. Encourage frequent use and replace when the stash runs low. Like any new habit you're trying to create, it will take a bit of time before thanking people becomes automatic. During team and one-on-one meetings, talk about who people on your team would like to recognize. Remind each other to hand out cards when the topic of someone helping out is brought up.

It's great feeling to find an envelope with your name on it propped on your keyboard.

Don't underestimate the power of a sincere and well-timed "Thank You". No need to wait for big accomplishments to share your gratitude. Tell people how much you appreciate them in a way they will remember. Lilly perks up when I say "Thank You", your colleagues will too.

Small tokens make a bit difference

Daily work is composed of activities ranging from large project deliverables to requests for information that only take a few seconds. Often, the work we planned to complete when we walked into the office is pushed aside for more urgent or unexpected requests. Most of us produce 50 - 100+ deliverables a week. These may be physical documents, answering questions, giving presentations, providing coaching, or a variety of other activities. All of these requests take time, and the planned activities don't just disappear while we are completing new work. It's difficult to keep morale high during the best of times, and is daunting when big change or stressful situations are impacting the organization.

During a particularly difficult project spanning 2

1/2 years, our project and UAT (user acceptance testing) teams were in a bit of a morale slump. The team had just learned our go live date would be pushed out three months, additional test scripts had to be written, and they were required to work the next six weekends to run scenario based testing. Ugh! We had to come up with a cost effective way to show these 50+ people that we understood they were stressed, and that their work was appreciated. We also wanted to add a bit of fun and brighten their days in the process. To satisfy the need for creative recognition that didn't break the bank, my colleagues and I turned to Pinterest and found brilliant ideas we could modify. After seeing how happy and energized employees were upon receiving the recognition, the decision was made to deliver a "Monday Morning Treat" every week until the system was live.

Design a clever note, add it to a colorful PowerPoint slide, attach with ribbon to a theme related snack, and you have fun way to recognize employees at a reasonable price. Listed below are a few adaptations to consider when looking for ways to show people their contributions are appreciated:

- GoldFish (individual box) - "You are O'FISHally the best team!"
- Rolo's and / or Tootsie Rolls - "We're on a ROLL to complete xxxx. Keep on rolling!"
- Extra Gum - "Thank you for your EXTRAordinary contribution to xxxx"
- Peppermint Patty and / or Junior Mints - "Your help last week MINT a lot!"
- Flipz pretzels - "This team FLIPZ out great work!"
- Popcorn microwave bag - "Just POPPED by to say thank you for xxx!"
- Reeses - "Have I told you REESEntly how much I appreciate you?"
- Use holidays and seasons:
  - Halloween: Themed bags filled with candy, stickers, plastic spiders, eyeball gum, and washable tattoo kits - "Project xxxx would be scary without you"
  - Thanksgiving: Pumpkin flavored homemade treat (include a turkey or pumpkin on the note) - "I'm thankful for your help on xxxx"
  - Candy Cane - "I CANE't imagine this project without you!"

There will always be people who think small rewards are silly and not necessary. Just remember, most people like to be recognized for their work and will appreciate the gesture. At the end of our project, one of the front line leaders walked up to me and said, "You know, we worked hard, there were some really tough and frustrating times during the project, but what I remember most is all of those little thank you treats your team handed out. I can recall almost every single one of them. Thank you for doing that." Genuine appreciation makes a difference. People will appreciate the time you took to make it special.

For those of you not familiar with Pinterest, it's a social network similar to Facebook in that each person has their own page and controls the content. Users create themed boards, and they "pin" images or videos to visually share with others. A board typically has a theme, and others can view and follow your boards. Like all social media sites, you control who can view your boards in the settings. It's free to join and you can find boards on just about any topic. You can find my "Rewards and Recognition" board containing over 40 pictures of examples similar to those detailed in this chapter at the following link:

https://www.pinterest.com/6sigmagirl/recognitio n-and-rewards/

Finding fun and creative ideas to recognize

colleagues and direct reports can be challenging, especially on a tight budget.

Here are six things to remember when showing appreciation:

Be specific - A generic "Thanks for all you do" doesn't feel sincere. In fact, vague expressions of gratitude can do more harm than good. Telling someone they wrote a great email, did a fantastic job on a deliverable, or provided superior support to a client is much more meaningful. The best praise is specific and includes a few details about how the contribution made a difference.

Act quickly - Say thank you as soon as you are aware of great work. The same day is best, within the week at a minimum. Don't wait until it's convenient for you to thank someone. Appreciation is about other people. Can you imagine how effective it would be if I waited until Lilly and I were home from a walk and said, "Thank you for healing so nicely by the lake, that's just the behavior I was looking for." Of course I wouldn't do that. Appreciation needs to be at the right time, and in a way that is meaningful to Lilly. The same rule applies to showing appreciation at work.

Show sincerity - Be genuine in your praise and explain why it mattered to your customers, the team, and you personally. Lilly knows from the tone of my voice and the look in my eye if my praise is genuine, people won't fall for false flattery either.

Appreciate progress - Don't wait for a job to be perfect to thank someone for hard work. Let employees know you appreciate them sticking with difficult tasks and recognize progress along the way.

Make it personal - You know the people you work with. Thank them in a way that will be meaningful to them. Some people like public praise and others prefer a private conversation. For one person an afternoon off is the best way to show gratitude, someone else might prefer a gift card to a local restaurant. Think about the people you are thanking and use what will be meaningful to them.

Bosses are people too - Don't forget to thank your boss and other leaders, they are often overlooked in the thank you department. This applies to front line managers as well as top executives. When an executive speaks at your kick-off, opens a training workshop, or removes significant roadblocks, spend a few minutes to write a thank you note. In addition to being the only card they receive that month (maybe that year or longer), your act of appreciation will be remembered and help to build a solid relationship.

Recognition and rewards are a necessary part of teaching Lilly how we want her to behave. When we give her a treat, pat on the head, or tell her "Thank you, Lilly" she is much more likely to continue being a good girl. The end result is that Jeff and I have a great dog we enjoy taking places and spending time with, and Lilly enjoys hanging out with us and gets positive attention everywhere we go.

Knowing how and when to recognize employees and coworkers is a leadership competency. As with any skill, you'll get better at it with practice. Showing appreciation will increase employee engagement, improve service to your customers, boost team morale, and it's a critical component to reinforcing change in your organization. On a personal level, it elevates your trustworthiness as a leader... plus it feels darn good!

CHAPTER FIVE

Consistency

Lilly:

"I get very frustrated when I can't figure out the rules!! When I was a puppy, I liked to grab dishcloths off of the counter. I knew my parents didn't like it by of the tone in their voices, but their instruction was so confusing!!! Sometimes they would yell "Off!", other times "Down!", and occasionally a stream of words I don't understand. One of the reasons this was so frustrating for me is that during obedience class I learned to lie at the command "Down". Using the same word for different instructions doesn't make sense. Luckily, my parents (with the help of our trainer) realized their directions caused me to be anxious and confused and they are much more consistent now. I'm really glad we have a trainer for my parents, they are behaving so much better!'"

Training Lilly:

Jeff and I were not consistent when we first started training Lilly. She was clearly confused, frustrated, and often didn't understand what we wanted her to do. Using different words for the action we wanted her to take was one problem, but there were others. When we were tired, it was sometimes easier to pretend she hadn't just taken the towel off the kitchen island again, or that she just darted by with a shoe in her mouth. Ignoring bad behavior certainly didn't make it go away. We were simply showing Lilly she could get away with things we didn't want her to do if she picked the right time. We also lacked diligence during walks. We enjoy evening walks, so after dinner we lace up our tennis shoes and go on a 4 - 6 mile walk around the neighborhood. What we don't enjoy is being taken for a walk by our dogs. After stopping for the 30th time in 20 minutes to stop Lilly from pulling (in case you think I'm exaggerating here, it really was that extreme), there were many times we just put up with the annoyance of being pulled along instead of correcting her behavior. No big surprise we weren't seeing the results we had hoped for. It was time to add consistency to Lilly's training regimen.

Lilly's Leadership Lesson:

Inconsistent leaders are immensely difficult to follow, and they generally lead by fear rather than trust. Be clear about what you want people to do, and never sway on the values or core principles that define your leadership style. Being consistent and providing clear direction will give your direct reports guardrails. People are able to make decisions and grow when they understand the mission of the organization and have a dependable leader guiding the team. Only then will employees take a few chances, make a few mistakes, and learn valuable lessons in the process. Consistent leadership is a cornerstone for trust, and you can't be a great leader without trust.

Being consistent takes work, especially when we are tired or under stress. When you find yourself turning a blind eye, take a step back and ask yourself if you're sending conflicting messages to your team, colleagues, and executive leadership on your values and priorities. Dependability is a skill. People perform better for trusted and steady leaders

If you say it, do it

Sounds simple, doesn't it? Yet we often find ourselves on the receiving end of broken commitments. In fact, it happens so frequently that sometimes we don't even realize it's happening. How many times have you had someone say, "We've got to get together for lunch soon" or "I'll give you call next week", and as they walk away you know you won't hear from them until the next chance meeting? Keeping commitments builds trust and relationships. Acting with integrity means keeping promises, and every commitment is a promise. Here are a few actions to help keep those promises:

Record commitments - I always keep a notebook with me to write down commitments. Capture all promises to ensure one doesn't slip from memory. We are all busy. It's easy to forget what we've agreed to do, especially the smaller things. Recording promises will help you remember them, and it feels good to mark off completed items!

Use technology - In addition to writing down your promises, record them electronically. Set reminders in your calendar at work or your smart phone. Set an alarm for immediate commitments you are in danger of forgetting.

Calendar events - Weekly desk calendars are great for recording meetings or those "to do" items that seem to never get done. Use these to jot down commitments as well.

Transfer responsibility - A commitment can become burden when you assume all of the responsibility. This is especially true when it comes to activities like scheduling lunch to catch up with busy colleagues. Send an email within a few days that includes date and time options. Even if a response isn't received, the commitment to take the lead on scheduling will have been met.

Communicate - Let people know when you run into trouble keeping a promise, the earlier the better! Never miss a meeting or due date without communicating why you aren't able to satisfy the original agreement, your recovery plan, and when it will be complete.

Say No - Saying no is a skill, and like all skills, proficiency will improve with practice. Making fewer promises makes it much easier to keep commitments. Here are a few tips on how to say no without damaging relationships:

- Set boundaries and offer alternatives - Let people know your boundaries and stick to them. I do a lot of networking and mentoring in the mornings, but I reserve evenings and weekends for my family. When I receive requests for dinner meetings, I'll politely decline and explain that evenings are reserved for my family. Then I'll suggest coffee or a conference call during my commute as an alternative. Boundaries often change over time. When my kids were young, I needed to be home in the morning to get them ready for school. At that time, my only networking options were lunch breaks or the occasional evening event.
- Ask for help prioritizing requests - This is especially helpful when saying no to your boss. Let your leader know you'd be glad to complete the assignment, but you'll need help deciding which of your other responsibilities can be deferred to a later due date or given to a team member.
- Solve the problem another way - Sometimes people ask for a specific action or deliverable that won't actually solve their problem. Offering an alternative solution can be a way of saying no while still meeting the need.

Be a Gift Giver

Give everyone a gift. It's not as weird as it first sounds. A gift can simply be sending the link to a website about a topic someone has expressed interest in. It may be forwarding job postings, or an article you suspect may be of interest. I recently received a fabulous gift from a woman I met at a Conscious Connections luncheon (Phoenix based leadership group). During the networking portion of the event I learned that one of the women at our table previously worked for a well-known publisher. As soon as she learned I was writing my first book, Julie whipped out her iPad and showed me the author podcasts she subscribes to. I couldn't believe how many free podcast series are available to help with the writing process, self-publishing, marketing, eBooks, print on demand, and the list goes on!! This woman gave me an amazing gift, and it didn't cost her a penny. This is what "give everyone a gift" is all about.

Listen closely during every conversation for a way you can add value. The right gift may not become apparent immediately. Don't be concerned, it's more important to share something of value later. Reaching out a few weeks after the initial introduction can have an even more powerful impact. Remembering someone is a form of flattery and shows the conversation or meeting was meaningful. Recognizing the perfect gift is easy when we listen fully and focus all of our attention on the person speaking. Gifts are always fun to receive, especially when one is completely unexpected. A few gifts that are easy and fun to give include:

- White papers
- Book recommendations
- Links to an upcoming conference
- Ted Talk videos or YouTube segments
- Articles (or links to articles) from Forbes, Fast Company, and other business publications
- Website links
- Connecting people in your network with shared interests
- Invitations to an event or networking opportunity
- LinkedIn invitations

There are also larger gifts you can give. These will generally be connected to an area of expertise or unique skill. Bigger gifts often require a significant personal time commitment. One example of a larger gift would be the offer to serve as a mentor. Because of my strong belief in the importance of mentorship, this is an area where I am a generous giver. There are ways to give liberally while maintaining boundaries. Be thoughtful about which rules of engagement work best in your situation and only give within those confines. A little bit of structure will create a positive giving experience for you and the recipient.

When the gift of sharing expertise is extended, there are many benefits for the giver as well. Mentoring is one activity where the person sharing expertise and information receives a great deal of value from the relationship. Through the experience of mentoring we expand our personal networks, learn about challenges in other industries or departments, and improve in the art of giving feedback. When we are very lucky, lifelong friends are made in the process.

I entered into a mentoring relationship with a woman named Stacey earlier this year. We met through a mutual connection on LinkedIn who thought our shared passion for change management would provide the foundation for great discussions. The remarkable thing about our relationship is the fact that we managed to meet at all because Stacey lives in Dubai, and I live in Arizona. We talk a few times a month about how she is navigating change in the local hotel industry, and I've had a front row seat in learning how the change management tools and assessments must be altered to fit the culture in Dubai. It's been a fantastic learning experience and I've met a lovely new friend.

Being a good gift giver is hard work. Here are a few helpful tips to ensure giving is a positive experience for you and the receiver:

Schedule meetings during personal time – Morning people may prefer to schedule coffee meetings before work. Those with long commutes might find time to take calls on the drive home. I'm not a fan of extra meetings after work because it would cut into my family time. Consider work and personal schedules to help set parameters that work best for your unique situation.

If you're a multitasking driver, please use a Bluetooth device or some other hands free technology. Nothing is more important than making it home safely.

Don't discuss private or sensitive company information – Unless something has been printed in the newspaper, or is easily available in a public forum, don't discuss your employer.

Don't share company assets – This includes physical material, documentation, or any other collateral. Assets belong to the company; they are not yours to give.

One last word of advice on this gift giving idea, it's really a promise. If you offer a gift, make a point to follow through. Don't say, "I read a great article about that last week, I'll send you the link", when you have no intention of doing so. Breaking promises will destroy trust and credibility. Only offer gifts you are willing and able to deliver. We're all busy, so make most gifts small and easy to deliver. Write down promises so you won't forget, and start giving freely!!

Gifts come back to you

Reciprocity is a form of karma. Cool things happen when we help people just because it's the right thing to do. Spectacular things happen to those who give without expectation of getting something in return.

An example of an unexpected gift happened when writing this book. It was an offer from Judy, a business professional I've been mentoring for several years. Now that probably conjures up images of long conversations and a structured meeting schedule, but nothing could be further from how our relationship works. Coaching can be as simple as a quick hallway conversation, a walk around the block to sort out an issue, or an occasional coffee chat. I shared with Judy that I was writing this book during one of our discussions, and she asked if I would allow her to edit the manuscript. I had been agonizing for months over how to find a good editor that fit in my budget. Judy appeared when I least expected it, and offered the gift of her editing talents.

For the next example we go back to Dubai. Stacey was my beta reader for this book. That's two amazing gifts that helped to make my dream of becoming an author a reality. There is a trick to receiving fabulous gifts that come at just the right time. Don't expect them, and be of assistance to others at every opportunity. The most cherished offer will likely be the gift of your time. Find ways to help others succeed and they will return the favor when you need it most.

Forming new habits

Change is hard. Replacing bad habits with desired behaviors can be daunting. This is especially true when it involves changing behaviors that come quite naturally, or better responses when under stress. I'm sure all of us have seen a less than desirable trait described in a leadership book and thought, "I've got to get better at (listening, giving feedback, delegating, etc.)". This is where focused practice and consistency are our best friends!

There are dozens of studies on how many days of practice it takes to form a new habit, but all studies have one thing in common… it's only a handful of days! When we practice a specific action or behavior for between 21 - 30 days in a row, it sticks and becomes part of our new routine. The trick is to be diligent in the frequency and length of time you rehearse new skills, and it's important to avoid skipping days in the initial 3 - 4 weeks. That sounds easy, but if you've ever tried to be a better listener, exercise regularly, or call your mom on a more frequent basis, you know how quickly old patterns sneak back into your daily routine. Here are a few tricks on how to make new habits stick:

Give it 30 days – After 30 days of practice, you will likely be proficient in the new behavior and it will have become part of your regular routine. Aiming for the higher end of the 21 - 30 days gives a few extra days to make the new behavior part of our regular routine.

20/20 vision – Be very clear in your vision, and why making this change is important. The reasons may involve benefits to your health, family life, career, or relationships. Write down the risks of not changing and benefits for your professional and family life. Use this information when you need motivation to instill new habits. Be sure to include answers to these questions when defining your change vision:

- Why do I feel this change is necessary?
- What is at risk if I don't make this change?
- Why is now the right time for me to change this habit?
- What exactly am I trying to change? (be very specific)
- What benefits will I realize by incorporating this new habit into my life?

Use reminders – We are creatures of habit, and many times we slip back into old behavior patterns without realizing it. Be strategic about how you remind yourself to act differently. A few ways to do this are:

- Use Post-it notes – Place these where you tend to slip back into old patterns. Perhaps on your bathroom mirror, computer screen, car steering wheel, calendar, pantry door, refrigerator, front door, or anywhere else a reminder would come in handy.
- Send yourself electronic messages – Add a calendar reminder (marked private and use "free time" scheduling), send yourself an email, or capture a note in an organization application. Add an event alarm for an additional cue.

- Wear a rubber band – Place a rubber band on your wrist and give it a gentle snap when you fall back into the old habit you are trying to break.
- Call a friend – Accountability partners can help keep us on track. This can be anything from asking a friend to go to the gym with you three times a week to a formal check in by phone on a regular cadence. Sharing your goals and progress will help keep motivation high when you're tempted to revert to the habit you're trying to break.
- Banish negative self-talk – We all fall victim to self-deprecating thoughts. Occasionally, the words actually come out of our mouths in conversation. I have a very good friend who doesn't allow this and has a funny way of stopping it almost the moment the words hit air. With a deadpan look, Kathy raises one hand and looks like she's erasing imaginary text in the air while she exclaims, "Erase, Erase, Erase!!!". Don't let negative self-talk creep in. Replace those thoughts with positive encouragement. Be diligent, as our inner critic shows up far too often.

Track goals – Set specific goals, then track progress and attainment. There are many methods you can use to keep yourself on track, use the one that works best for you. My preference is to track progress to goals on a large calendar. It hangs in my pantry and each day I jot down activities completed that relate to daily exercise and writing goals. I'm much more likely to sit down and edit a manuscript or go for a long walk when part of my routine is to record progress at the end of the day.

Be your own best friend – You don't expect your best friend to be perfect, so give yourself a break! We aren't perfect, so when you struggle during the change process that simply means you're human. If you slip, get back up and begin again. This is a time when negative self-talk shows up, so be ready with encouraging replacement messages!

Reward yourself – Don't wait until you've achieved a goal to enjoy a reward. Small rewards along the way will help sustain new habits. Treating yourself well is a great habit to incorporate into your life! Decide how you will celebrate your success and follow through.

What gets measured gets done

The saying, "What gets measured gets done" has been attributed to Peter Drucker, Edward Deming, Tom Peters, and several other organizational and improvement gurus. While the origin of the quote is not certain, the message is clear... if you expect a change to stick, or a set of behaviors to permeate throughout the culture of your organization, find a way to measure it. Measuring performance is only possible when leaders are clear and set stable expectations. That requires consistent leadership.

Starting with a well-defined vision on how your team will support customers and colleagues is the place to start. Even better, set up a workshop that includes direct reports and set the vision together. When people participate in creating what the future will look like, they are more engaged, and will clearly understand where the guardrails are. Employees feel more empowered to make decisions when boundaries and expectations are clear. Additionally, innovative and creative ideas flourish when teams collaborate to create the future.

Try holding a team workshop to set the course for what will be accomplished over the next 12 months. I've had good results planning these sessions just before the start of each fiscal year. The activities change a bit year to year, but the basic format stays the same. These planning sessions generally run about six hours. All team members are invited to attend, and we always hold them in a conference room at the office.

While we enjoy the occasional offsite meeting, I want the team to be creative and excited in the office. Innovation should happen where we work, not only when we take a trip to a different location.

Topics covered in our planning session include:

- Review and refinement of the team vision (three years out)
- Brainstorming on the enablers and detractors to achieving the vision
- Gaps in the business our team can fill
- Training the team needs
- What we are most proud of from the previous year
- What we want customers and colleagues to say about our team at the close of the coming fiscal year

After the framework has been developed, decide the best way to measure what will be accomplished. Goals should be realistic and limited to no more than five. Revisit measurements in team meetings, and discuss each persons' contribution to the team goal during one-on-one sessions. It's motivating when goals are displayed in a common area, so find a place to post the goal and track attainment. Make these displays colorful and easy to follow. Lastly, don't forget to celebrate milestones and when the goal is reached.

Indecisive leaders don't set meaningful goals because targets are constantly changing. Consistency provides a safe framework for teams to achieve goals and take well-calculated risks.

Lilly is a lot more fun to be around when our directions are clear and consequences are predictable. She knows the boundaries and does a pretty good job of staying within them. She is more confident in her actions because she knows what is allowed, and I think our gal is happier with consistent rules.

If you've ever worked for a boss who seemed to have a personality disorder, you know the importance of consistency first hand! Early in my career, I worked for a confusing leader named Josh. He could be collaborative and supportive one day, and the next morning he would be snide and offensive. I never knew which Josh would show up to work! It caused a great deal of stress for the team and a tentative approach to issues. Many times, team concerns and mistakes were hidden. We never knew how he would react, or which "Josh" would show up for work. Don't be a Josh. Your team deserves better, and you do too.

CHAPTER SIX

Patience

Lilly:

"I can tell when my mom is irritated and it makes me extremely nervous. When I feel anxious, it's hard to listen and I make a lot of mistakes. I know when my mom is mad, but I get frustrated too, and that makes it difficult for me to get back into training mode. It's so much easier to do what mom wants me to when she is calm, relaxed, and nice to be around. It's no fun taking direction from someone who is mad, frustrated, or uptight."

Training Lilly:

When I'm frustrated with Lilly, it has a visibly negative effect on her behavior. Even when I work hard at controlling my voice and reactions, she senses when my anxiety is on the rise. The more frustrated I become, the less obedient Lilly is, and the cycle continues. I'm getting better at recognizing when I'm the one who needs an attitude adjustment. It's challenging to transition from feeling exasperated to being a calm and patient leader, but the benefits are certainly worth the effort. It's amazing to watch Lilly's outlook improve right along with mine!

While there is value in masking frustration (the "fake it 'till you make it approach), finding a way to quickly return to a place of true understanding and composure is far more effective. Unless you are an academy award-winning actor, your direct reports know when you are frustrated with them or the situation at hand. Learning to control our emotions is a much better option. Better decisions are made when stress levels are low, and we deal with issues more effectively.

Lilly's Leadership Lesson:

It's a terrible feeling when you know colleagues and leaders are frustrated with you, especially when you are giving your best effort. Many times these negative feelings cause us to make mistakes, and the vicious cycle starts... the more mistakes you make the worse you feel, the worse you feel the more mistakes you make, and the spiral continues. Finding a way to show patience gives people the room they need to relax and improve their performance. Higher levels of patience are valuable when training new hires, implementing new systems or processes, or coaching employees on behavior changes. Those you lead will make more successful transitions, team morale will improve and the workday will become much more enjoyable for everyone.

Build Trust

Patience and trust are tightly linked. Demonstrating patience and encouragement is necessary to grow trust. While we don't often see these attributes linked, it's hard for one to exist without the other. The dictionary defines trust as believing someone is "reliable, good, honest, and effective". When trust is the foundation of work relationships, we have no doubt that employees are doing their very best. Trusted leaders are focused on removing barriers and finding ways to help direct reports succeed. On those days when patience is running low in the tank, take a moment to ask if your focus on trust has slipped a bit. Chances are it has. With a bit more focus on trust you'll find you relax and your patience grows in the process.

111

Timing is important

I used to think Lilly was much easier to train in the morning and on weekends. She seemed to be more relaxed and attentive than in the evenings when I returned from work. She was not lonely during the day or cooped up in her kennel while I was away. Jeff is retired so he's home with her all day, and she has plenty of attention while I'm gone. I couldn't figure out why the training experience varied so much and yielded such different results. Well, as it turns out the difference has very little to do with Lilly and a lot to do with me. I am much more relaxed and energetic in the early morning, and this certainly true on the weekends. When my mind is relaxed I'm a better trainer for Lilly, so of course she responds better!

Knowing when you perform your best is a great bit of information to use to your advantage. When possible, leaders should to plan difficult or sensitive activities for those times when their attention and patience is the highest. Because I know the time of day when I am most patient and able to give full attention, I plan these activities during earlier hours of the day whenever possible:

Coaching moments - I use the phrase "coaching moment" to describe a desired change in behavior, or observation of something that I'm concerned about. These are not punitive discussions. Feedback is intended to be helpful and to provide insight into a different way to handle a situation or issue.

One-on-One's - I meet with direct reports each week to find out how they are doing and where they need my help. I also use this time to find out what they need me to start, stop, or continue doing in my support. Especially when seeking performance feedback, select a time when your patience tank is full.

Difficult tasks - Schedule those difficult or thought provoking activities for the time of day when you are refreshed and feeling most focused. It may be helpful to add a meeting to your calendar. If I don't plan and reserve thinking time, something else usually fills my most productive part of the day.

Crucial conversations - Difficult conversations cause anxiety and drain our energy. When you suspect a discussion is likely to be emotional, controversial, or downright unpleasant, be thoughtful about the best time of day to begin the dialogue. Of course we can't always anticipate when a conversation will turn crucial, but when you can, a bit of planning will improve your delivery and the outcome.

Look through the data lens

When emotions are high, opinions vary, and patience is low, data becomes your best friend! Bringing data to the conversation is the quickest and most impactful way to remove emotion and move to meaningful dialogue. Even subjective data reduces tension. Facts help change the course of the conversation toward finding solutions vs. pointing fingers and placing blame. Knowing what data to collect or look at isn't always easy. Sometimes it's sitting in a database just waiting for someone to look at it with fresh eyes. The next time you're anticipating a difficult conversation, use a few facts to get people in a patient mindset. Here are a few places to look data to focus conversations and reduce emotions:

Surveys - Most companies have some sort of employee satisfaction and customer experience survey process. The data is generally fairly easy to get access to, especially when you make it clear that your intent is to suggest actions based on the results. Look through the answers and comments to mine facts and popular opinion that relate to your topic.

Assessments - These are really mini surveys. Make them short and to the point. Perhaps all you need is two or three questions and a text box for comments. Think carefully about what you really want to know. Using the right wording for questions can be tricky. Design the survey, and then ask a few trusted colleagues to review the assessment and provide feedback. They can help ensure that the questions would return the information you need.

Interviews - This is really just a verbal assessment. When collecting information via interview, follow the assessment advice. The conversations may lead to additional questions; however, it's important to start with a standard set to keep your findings consistent and relevant. When possible, keep the interviews short. Most people can fit an extra 10 - 15 minutes into their day. Tell interview participants how long it will take and stick to the agreed upon time.

Take notes - Some data is as simple as walking around and writing down what you see. Observe how work is being completed, take notes, and turn them into data!

System usage - Request system usage reports to learn how many people are using a system, how often certain screens are accessed, and how product and services are flowing.

Tick marks - If there is a need to know how often something is occurring in a process, ask a few people to record the event during their day. This can be as simple as marking tick marks on paper. The data is easy to collect, current, and involves people working in the process in discovery. A few words of caution: be sure to let employees know this is a temporary request, be specific on what you want them to count, and make the data collection period short. Typically you'll only need them to collect information for a week or so.

A few words of caution when conducting surveys and assessments:

Avoid survey fatigue - Be thoughtful about when you ask people to participate. If your company tends to send a lot of surveys, look into the possibility of combining what you need to know with an existing questionnaire. Soliciting feedback is important, but overdoing these requests can be tiresome.

Tell people the results, then do something about it - Only survey people who you intend to share the results and next steps with. Employees feel good about spending time giving thoughtful responses when their feedback drives positive change.

Mine comments for additional data - Comments are a goldmine of information that is often overlooked. In fact, this is often where you'll find the most interesting and actionable data! Create an Excel spreadsheet and add the comments in the first column. Then, add categories in the following columns with topics mentioned in the comments. Comments may include multiple topics, so expect to score some comments with more than one "x". All you've got to do is put an "x" in the column where the topic is mentioned, create a quick pivot table, and you'll see the data in a new and interesting way.

During those times that I find myself wishing Lilly would settle down or behave better, I've learned it's time to work on my own patience. My anxiety and frustration level has a lot to do with her self-confidence and attitude. Pretending I'm not exasperated is a good first step, but our gal is quite savvy and figures out that I'm faking it pretty quickly. Lilly is more relaxed and obedient when I am patient and calm.

The amount of patience a leader shows has a big impact on team culture. Patient leaders listen carefully, use data to defuse tense conversations, celebrate mistakes and what is learned from them, and see situations from others point of view. They encourage honesty and seek feedback to improve their performance, decisions impacting the team, and work processes. Working on being a more patient leader will increase trust and open the door to learning that cannot happen when patience is missing. All you have to do is think about a leader you've worked with who lacked this quality to know why it's an important one to cultivate.

Increasing patience will reduce stress for you and your team, improve your decision-making, increase the amount of information and feedback you receive, and bump up your personal trust score. That's a pretty good return for your patience investment!

CHAPTER SEVEN

Fun!

Lilly:

"My parents have always done a lot of training with me, but sometimes a girl just wants to have fun!! Mom and I work on commands every morning before she leaves for work, but today I wasn't in the mood. My favorite things to do are going for long walks, closing kitchen drawers, playing hide and seek with my favorite toy, and running with my friends at the dog park. I enjoy all of the time we spend together, even training time, but too much training doesn't help me learn. When my parents don't play with me enough I'll find my own fun ... and that isn't good for any of us!"

Fun with Lilly:

Jeff and I love dogs. They have always been a part of the family and I can't imagine our home without the pitter-patter of little paws on the tile floor. A good, well-behaved dog is certainly more fun to have around the house, but they also need to have fun, exercise, and spend time relaxing with the family. It's hard to remember this when chasing your beloved pet around the house to retrieve a dishtowel or your favorite leather pump. If I don't build in enough fun time for Lilly, she won't be on her best behavior. Her fun time includes trips to the dog park, long walks, fetch, laser tag games, and relaxing on the couch with us. We are definitely sneaking in a bit of training and reinforcement during some of these fun activities, but to Lilly, it just feels like a break. She is much happier and better able to work hard on learning new skills when the right amount of amusement is built into her day.

Have fun with your team! If you aren't enjoying your time at work, it will feel like drudgery and creativity will suffer. Laugh, smile, and build fun into every day. You'll be happier and so will your team.

Lilly's Leadership Lesson:

Finding creative ways to build fun into the workplace improves morale, increases quality and productivity, and best of all… makes work fun for everyone! People will work harder and achieve more when they enjoy coming to work every day. I once heard Jack Welch speak at a conference and his simple trick really hit home… if you want to do great things at work, people must want to "hang with you". This requires us to create an environment like the cool kids' basement in high school, which means everyone will want to be on your team. People won't hesitate to ask your group for support because your team delivers high quality, has a reputation of approachability, and they are known for enjoying their work. The most talented employees will look for opportunities to work for you, and the most valuable projects will come your way when you are the "cool kids".

Fun alone won't turn your team into the "cool kids' basement" of your organization, but it's certain the team won't get there without it!

Take a break

A break in the action is often the best antidote to frustration. When beginning to feel exasperated, offended, or just down right angry, that should be the clue that it's time to take a break. Your timeout might be as simple as delaying your response to an email that has you riled, or as dramatic as taking a long overdue vacation. Taking a step back improves our ability to manage stressful situations. By setting the example, others will be encouraged to do the same. Sometimes that's all it takes to restore patience and move stressful situations from chaos to calm. I'll be the first to admit I don't take breaks often enough. It takes a lot of discipline to build rest into a busy schedule. Remember, direct reports will follow your lead. If you don't take time to reenergize during the day, they won't either. Here are a few ways to build breaks into you day:

Go for a walk - If the weather is cooperating, get outside for some fresh air! When old man winter or extreme heat makes it difficult to enjoy the outdoors, head to a local mall and take a 20-minute stroll. If there is a company warehouse or other large work facility near the office, gather the team for a tour. Finding a "Break Buddy" can help make taking a break a standard part of the day. A quick stretch or walking break a few times each day gets the blood flowing, warms up tired muscles, and leaves us feeling refreshed.

Take a lunch break - This doesn't mean sitting at your desk consuming a diet Dr. Pepper and a bag of pretzels from the vending machine. I'm talking about going to the break room or cafeteria, or leaving the building to enjoy a meal. I'm totally guilty of fitting in a quick bite (hence the soda and pretzels comment) in between meetings. That is certainly not a healthy way to treat your body on many levels. When I do walk away from my desk to enjoy a meal, it is refreshing and my work will be better after the short break. Take your 30 - 60 minutes for lunch. I bet you'll accomplish the same amount of work during the day and feel better in the process.

Read a book - Taking 20 minutes to read a chapter of a good book is a nice break from reality. It can be a business book from your to do list or that novel you've been dying to read. Reading often takes us to another world. This quick mental break may be just what is needed to energize your day.

Be creative - Sketch, color, write (blog, book, white paper, poem), or something else that will help to tap into your creative side. We all have one! Write a blog, white paper, or spend 20 minutes jotting down ideas for that book you've had rattling around in your head. Satisfy your inner muse by sketching. There is a pack of crayons sitting on my desk for those times when I need a creative boost. When I'm feeling stuck, I simply open the pack and smell them. There is something about the scent of my youth that wakes up my creative muse. Indulge in a bit of fun that increases creativity.

Treat yourself - Stop by your favorite coffee shop for a midday treat or go to the grocery store to pick up healthy snacks for the week. Find a place close to the office where you can get a manicure or massage during lunch. Call a good friend or supportive family member you don't talk to often enough.

Take a vacation - We need our vacations in a desperate way! I can't tell you how many people I know who never take a vacation, or they take them so infrequently that they actually loose earned time off. Don't lose vacation! Always plan for your time off, and make it a true break by unplugging from work. You'll be amazed at how much better you feel. Work will move forward without you, and your family will appreciate the undivided attention.

Work Differently

Work is, well… a lot of work! We are all under pressure to produce high quality products and services in the most efficient way, but that doesn't mean all work must be done in a traditional way. The best time to build in a bit of fun at work is long before patience runs low, teams are frustrated, and you find yourself spending the majority of your day on damage control. That doesn't mean you shouldn't infuse some fun at these critical times, just don't make the mistake of forgetting about fun when times are good. Finding different ways to accomplish standard activities is a breath of fresh air!!!

Walking team meetings - This is especially nice during the months when your area enjoys beautiful weather. Walking meetings work best with small groups of 3 - 7, with any more than 10 people, it's difficult to engage in meaningful conversations. These shouldn't be structured meetings, just take a walk and get to know your team better. Find out what people love about their jobs, what they would like to start doing for your customers, or just chat about what people are going to do for the coming weekend. Sometimes I'll suggest we talk about work for 30 minutes. Work is off limits for the second half of the outing. It's amazing how relaxed and energized the team is when we are back at our seats an hour later. Give it a try. The results may be surprising!

Team builders - Schedule something fun for the team at least once a quarter. It doesn't have to be big, just fun. Of course, if you have a big team it can be challenging to find an activity everyone puts in the fun category. Ask for suggestions from the group for future events and alternate the types of activities. Consider rotating the responsibility to organize team builders. Do your best to plan events all employees are able to participate in. Even the grumpiest people will appreciate your efforts.

Volunteer - Find a non-profit the team would like to support and schedule time to help out. Many companies provide a set number of hours employees can use each year to volunteer. If your company offers this benefit, be sure to take advantage of it. Some of the things you may want to consider include:

- Assist with serving meals at a local homeless shelter. If it's not possible to serve during the lunch hour, ask people if they'd like to meet in the morning before work for the breakfast shift.

- Work with a non-profit to collect donations for an upcoming event.
- Organize an internal fundraiser - Food drops, clothing drives, and school supply drives are a few examples. Many times the benefiting organization will supply posters and drop boxes. Our team organized a huge candy gram event that raised over 7K for a local non-profit that provides education to families at risk. One warning here is that these internal campaigns can be quite time consuming, so be sure your leadership team is in full support of using work time for the planning and execution of the event.

Hold offsite 1:1's - I have weekly one-on-one meetings with my direct reports. Before our meeting, they document high-level discussion times on a standard form. I use the form as a discussion guide, and after the meeting I'll add details about our conversation. These notes typically include information about the status of projects or assignments, coaching suggestions, and what employees need from me to be successful. The data on the forms are good resources for performance reviews, documenting decisions, and agreed upon next steps. A quick comment about taking notes, don't type them during the discussion. It's OK to quickly jot down a few things, but don't write an essay during the one-on-one. These one-hour meetings are dedicated to listening. Trust is built by looking at people, not the computer.

One-on-ones should be structured, but that doesn't mean they have to be stiff or formal. One way to build in a bit of fun is to have these meetings offsite... here are a few places that work very well:

- Coffee Shop - Venues with nice outside seating areas are best. Again, this is a nice break during lovely weather. When outside or in a quiet place away from the office, people tend to open up a bit more. The ambiance makes a big difference. Search for fun locations near your office and give it a try.
- Restaurants - Again, outside is always nice... but if this isn't possible, choose a place that has quiet space you can talk. We usually take an hour for the 1:1, and then take an hour for lunch. Work discussion during lunch is not allowed! Usually...
- Park - A green space with comfortable seating is a great place to talk. If you're lucky enough to have a great outdoor space within walking distance from your office be sure to use it!

If you like the idea of including a form to guide weekly meetings with your folks, be creative and include topics that are important to you and your team.

Here are the categories included on the form my team uses:

- Date
- Overall, I think I'm:
  [ ] Doing OK   [ ] Overloaded

  [ ] Frustrated   [ ] On top of things

  [ ] Snowed under, but I'll be okay in _____ days or so

- I am waiting on you for the following:
- I have made progress on these performance goals:
- Information / News, etc.:
- Recommendations:
- Highlights, for me, in the last week / month:
- Mistakes I want to celebrate:

Just for Fun

Laughing is good for us. It improves our mood and sense of wellbeing, so build a bit of silly fun into your day. A few ways to include a fun into work include:

Contests - Set-up contests, and think of fun ways to include the children and grandchildren of employees. Find creative ways to engage everyone. A few contests I've seen be very successful include:

- Art contests for children - The winning selections can be used as office decorations, art for holiday cards, or artwork for the company calendar.
- Photo contests for employees – The options for art contest above apply here.
- Hold a bake-off - Make it competitive and watch the fun begin! Perhaps every dish must contain a certain ingredient, something like pumpkin during the Thanksgiving holiday or cinnamon at Christmas time. (Yes, I just said Christmas, and I'm not going to apologize for it... that's one of the perks of writing your own book!). The prize for the winning dish? A trinket the winner proudly displays on their desk until next year's competition.

Book Fairs - Arrange to have a book fair in your cafeteria or common area. Local bookstores, especially local independent shops, often welcome this type of opportunity.

Arts and Craft Fairs - There is amazing hidden talent within your organization! Create the opportunity for employees to bring handcrafted items for sale and you'll be amazed at the artistic ability of your co-workers. Christmas time (yep, I did it again) is a great time to run a craft fair. It's an opportunity for employees to purchase handmade gifts, and employees can earn a little extra money in the process. Everyone wins!

Veterans Day Activities - Coordinate an event to write thank you notes to veterans serving in our armed forces.

Ice Cream Socials - Who doesn't love an ice cream social? Organize a root beer float or ice cream sundae social. Include a few healthier options like frozen yogurt or sorbet.

Halloween Contest - Create a fun competition with small prizes for the scariest, funniest, and most original costumes. Team themed contests can be great team builders. Throw in a cube-decorating contest and you have yourself the makings for a fun party!

Employee Day - I've seen this set-up during a workday for employees, or on Saturday as a family event. Either way, taking a day to recognize and thank employees is a great morale booster. If you can swing nice raffle prizes, it adds a bit more excitement to the day.

Diversity Potluck - Ask people to bring dishes to celebrate their heritage. It's a great way to learn about other cultures, and employees enjoy sharing family recipes.

Recipe Sharing - Speaking of family recipes, create a company cookbook. It can be an online book or something that is printed for distribution. Ask people to add a picture of the person who created the dish, or of the family cooking together.

Baby Picture Contest - Ask everyone on your team to bring in a baby picture. Post them in a common area and have a contest to see who can guess the identity of the babies. The person with the most correct answers wins a prize.

Don't take it too far

Use caution and good sense when infusing a bit of play into the workday. Fun without caution could lead to hurt feelings or in the worst cases, a visit with a HR representative to explain your "good idea". Keep these things in mind when planning the next lighthearted diversion for your team:

Jokes are dangerous - Notice I didn't say "don't tell jokes". Do be careful. Off color jokes and innuendos are NEVER a good idea. Also be careful when using sarcasm, especially when working with people from other countries. Because it doesn't translate well, the use of sarcasm is often offensive or confusing.

Choose activities carefully - It's no fun to be left out or forgotten. Structure activities in a way that everyone feels invited and welcome to participate. Some will opt out, and that's OK. Extend the invitation and let employees decide how and when they want to participate.

After hours fun - Use caution with alcohol. I've included more detail on this in the networking chapter. As a general rule, go ahead and enjoy a drink, maybe two if the event lasts several hours, then stop drinking. You'll never regret not indulging in drink number three; however, regrets will rise exponentially with your drink count. This is definitely when the "better safe than sorry" advice is a perfect fit.

Be inclusive - Make sure the fun includes everyone. Constant side jokes and banter between two or three people is only fun for those included in the conversation. Mingle and chat to pull everyone into the fun. You don't want an environment where people feel like they don't belong.

Fun at the expense of others - Mean spirited comments and making fun of others is never OK. I've had people I coach say to me "It wasn't funny, so I just stayed quiet until they started talking about something else". There is no good excuse for participating; the listener is just as guilty as the speaker! Worse, everyone who hears the conversation or learns about it will now associate you with the ugly things said. Never participate in mean spirited or negative conversations. They are career killers.

Questionable fun - We've all been there, that awkward moment when a conversation takes a turn we are not comfortable with. The subject is usually sexual, religious, or other inappropriate content. Our feet feel like they are rooted in cement while our brain is telling us to run. While the person telling an off color-joke is talking, your brain is trying to figure out if you should leave or stay, and then suddenly it's too late. The punch line has been delivered and you are guilty by association. The solution? Remove yourself at the onset of the dialogue. It's easier than you might think. Simply smile and say "I'm really not comfortable with off-color jokes, so I'm going to remove myself from the conversation. Enjoy the rest of your day and I'll talk with you later". It's that easy! People will respect you for leaving the conversation, and doing it in a way that doesn't pass judgment on others. You'll feel better, your integrity and professionalism will be elevated, and it's an opportunity to show others a path to better decisions in the future.

Play is such an important part of our lives, and Lilly reminds me every day to slow down and have fun. In fact, fun is part of our training strategy! When we know that we will be going to an outdoor cafe for a bite to eat where Lilly will need to show exceptional manners, our first stop is to the dog park for a long play session. The fact that she is tired is a bonus, but more importantly, she enjoyed her playtime and is ready to get to work.

Remember what Jack Welch says, your team has to be like the cool kids basement from high school… people have to want to "hang with you"! If you aren't having a good time at work, finding different ways to do work, and building breaks into the day, nobody is going to want hang out with you or your team. Sweatshops aren't fun. Creativity and innovation won't thrive in that environment.

On the flip side, fun can have the opposite intended effect. In the worst case, it can be the reason for an uncomfortable trip to HR, and nobody wants to be involved in that!

CHAPTER EIGHT

Conclusion

Brilliant leaders are patient, consistent, thoughtful, and kind. They communicate clearly, set expectations and provide training and coaching. When change is introduced, the best leaders are involved and tirelessly tie the reason for the change to the vision and strategy of the company. We trust brilliant leaders because they build amazing teams that have fun while delivering value to the organization. Perhaps most importantly, brilliant leaders remember that processes, metrics, and goals are fueled by people who will do just about anything for a leader who recognizes accomplishments, cares about people, and isn't afraid to celebrate mistakes along the way.

I love being Lilly's dog mom. When she joined our family there was no doubt I'd enjoy her championship, but I had absolutely no idea Lilly would become my leadership coach. If she could talk, Lilly would tell you the training is going well. I'm making progress and having a lot of fun in the process. I'm sure Lilly has many more lessons to teach me. Becoming a brilliant leader is a never-ending journey, and I wouldn't have it any other way.

Now that you've heard from me... I'd love to hear from you!

I would really appreciate it if you would leave a review and share your thoughts on this book. Your feedback helps other readers find books that match their interests, and I'm looking forward to learning how to be a better writer from your comments and suggestions. Becoming a brilliant leader is a lifelong journey. Thank you for being part of mine.

About Carla

Carla Howard is a successful international change leader and coach. She is a respected speaker, mentor, and change consultant. Carla lives in Phoenix, Arizona. In her free time, she enjoys spending time with her family and traveling during the summer months to escape the Arizona heat!

Carla can be found on:

EMAIL: Carla@TheProfessionalWomansMentor.com

INSTAGRAM: TheProfessionalWomansMentor

TWITTER: Mentor4Women

LINKEDIN: Carla Howard

Acknowledgements

No author writes a book alone. I am incredibly fortunate to have parents who love and believe in their children fiercely, and have always told my sister and I that we can be and do anything we desire. My children, grandchildren, and extra kids (you know who you are) have added immense joy to my life. I've learned so much from them, and I am incredibly proud of the young adults they have become.

In the book Lean In, Sheryl Sandberg talks about how important it is for young women to choose a supportive husband. She's taken a lot of criticism for that advice, but from my point of view, Sheryl is 100% right. Jeff Howard has been my best friend, confidant, and sounding board for almost 14 years. He believes in me, supports my dreams, and makes me laugh out loud every day. My life is infinitely more grounded, balanced, and fun because he is in it.

Carla Howard

141